Mission and Ministry

Mission and Ministry

Adrian Hastings

Sheed and Ward · London and Sydney

First published 1971
Sheed and Ward Ltd, 33 Maiden Lane, London WC2E 7LA, and
Sheed and Ward Pty Ltd, 204 Clarence Street, Sydney NSW 2000

Nihil obstat : J. M. T. Barton, D.D., Censor
Imprimatur : + Victor Guazzelli, Vicar General
Westminster, 4 November 1970

SBN 7220 0619 5

This book is set in Linotype Baskerville

Made and printed in Great Britain by
William Clowes and Sons, Limited
London, Beccles and Colchester

CONTENTS

CONTENTS

PREFACE

Mission and Ministry is offered as a sequel to *Church and Mission in Modern Africa*. It is intended to throw further light upon a number of aspects of the missionary apostolate at a very critical moment and upon the growth of the church in Africa today. I hope that most of what is said will be of concern to people everywhere for the future both of missionary organisation and of the church in Africa are truly major matters for the church universal. In particular two themes emerge: one is the theological necessity behind christian participation in the contemporary struggle for social, political and economic justice; the second is a positive approach to a radical restructuring of the church's own ordained ministry at a time when the accustomed pattern is crumbling upon every side.

Much of the thinking for this book was done during my fifteen months stay at Mindolo Ecumenical Foundation in Zambia and I am very glad to acknowledge here the stimulus I owe to many good friends at Mindolo and to the ideals of christian worldliness which the Foundation has always endeavoured to express.

Adrian Hastings

ACKNOWLEDGEMENTS

Chapter 1 was first prepared as a lecture for the Irish National Mission Week, held at Navan in September 1968, and later appeared in *The Church is Mission*, Geoffrey Chapman. Chapter 2 was published in the *Clergy Review* for March 1966. Chapter 4 originated as a lecture delivered at a study weekend in Dar es Salaam, August 1967, and was later published in a booklet entitled *The Arusha Declaration and Christian Socialism* by the Tanzania Publishing House. Chapter 6 first appeared in *Race: A Christian Symposium* edited by C. S. Hill and D. Mathews and published by Victor Gollancz. Chapter 7 was in the *Month* for April 1958. Chapter 8 was written for *Concilium*, March 1969. Chapter 9 has appeared in five numbers of the *African Ecclesiastical Review* from April 1969 to April 1970. Chapter 10 started as a lecture for a Makerere study week and was published, June 1969, in *Zeitschrift für Missionwissenschaft u. Religionswissenschaft*. An earlier draft of chapter 11 was written as a position paper for the 1969 Seminar Study Year of the Church in Tanzania. My thanks to all concerned for permission to republish. All the chapters have been very considerably rewritten before appearing here.

1

THE MISSIONARY TODAY AND TOMORROW

The absolute aim of missionary work to reveal Christ through his body the church to those who do not know him does not change. It will always be an integral combination of witness and service, the two together building up a believing fellowship. But immediate aims, methods of work and organisation, the type of training required, can and do vary greatly according to the needs of the church and world in each age and place. It is evident that priorities in mission in, say, 1950 were very different from those in 1900. It is clear again that the whole type of work possible and desirable has always been vastly different in, for example, the Congo and India, and the work in either has been very different from that possible in Algeria. Again, Japan has presented quite another problem.

If the church is the sacrament of Christ, and the specific purpose of missionary work is to make the church explicitly present and vital within a particular group of the human family, a human community limited in terms of space and time, a community in which hitherto Christ's ecclesial presence has not been effective; then its material character must depend upon the here and now condition of that particular human community. Moreover, as missionary work is human work—the limited activity of a certain number of people—one has also constantly to judge what is feasible and should take priority in terms of the number and capacities of those whom God has called to the task.

As the same sort of questions, born of the same pressures,

arise in place after place, it is plain that the answers—or the principles behind the answers—have to be formulated at far more than local level. What should the church of today and the missionary of today consider paramount in the missionary task? There is still no one answer to such a question. Even where different countries or local churches are clearly moving in somewhat the same direction, they may still be doing so at different speeds and may, furthermore, at any particular moment be at very different places on the road.

From some points of view, it is surely true that the churches of Asia are some fifteen years further along the road than those of Africa. The fact that political independence came to most countries of Asia in the late 1940s, but to those of Africa in the early 1960s may not be very significant by the year 2000, but it does make a great difference now. Thus the indigenisation of the episcopate has, to date, gone much less far in Africa than in Asia.[1] The attitude of most African governments to admitting foreign missionary personnel is still far more open than that of many Asian governments, and so on. Yet the general direction in which the situation is moving is much the same, and what is true today for Asia will soon be true also for Africa.

In other things, however, the situation of most local churches in these two continents is indeed different and the effect of these differences on missionary priorities ought to be very considerable. Perhaps the greatest difference of all is that—apart from the Philippines—the churches in Asia are relatively small in numbers and are growing slowly, if at all. Moreover, many of them have traditions going back several hundred years. The missionary coming to Africa or, for that matter, to the Philippines or to South America, enters almost everywhere into a church of vast numbers

---

[1] One is obliged to note sadly here the ecclesial scandal that the indigenisation of the episcopate in Africa is being carried out only in black ruled countries. Though the vast majority of Catholics in South Africa, Rhodesia, Angola and Mozambique are black, there is not a single diocesan black bishop in those four countries at the time of writing.

with a continual and very rapid increase in nominal Catholics. In practice this basic numerical fact is of decisive importance in shaping the immediate efforts of church workers.

This is coupled with a second fact. Whereas most of the Asian churches have a relatively large number of local priests, most of the churches of Africa have very few in proportion to their size, and the position is hardly improving. It can be said that as regards numbers and ministry, Africa is moving only too rapidly in a direction already taken by the church in South America. But of course on other points there are vast differences between these two continents resulting both from past history and the present economic situation.

Again, the position in regard to non-christian religions is not the same. On this point Africa stands somehow between Asia and South America. In Asia the church has always been confronted with great religious traditions—buddhism, hinduism, islam—and their strength has greatly limited her growth. Compared with them the church in Asia has too often appeared as a ghetto for those with particular European connections and her first duty now is a new approach to the great religions and their adherents within a specifically Asiatic context. In Africa the position has been different. Islam indeed is strong and some of the traditional religions too are showing great powers of survival, but missionaries have largely ignored the former—sometimes to their cost—and the willingness of millions of other people to become christian has so absorbed missionary energies that there has been little thought for anything else. Today in Africa there is a real need for a new and deeply sympathetic approach to non-christian religions, but it cannot be said that this need has the same priority in Africa as in Asia. In South America non-christian religious traditions do not exist on a large scale.

It is impossible to combine the needs of such extremely different situations in a single study. Indeed it appears to me that one of the very greatest failings of the missionary endeavour in the past, and even still today, is precisely this: to consider that there is in practice a single missionary task for which men can be prepared in a single general way. The fact that societies could train men indiscriminately for work in quite different fields, and only after ordination and the completion of a six year training course decide where they should go—to Japan, to India, to Tanzania—seems to indicate a basically misguided, because terrifyingly over-simplified, view of missionary work. Nevertheless today it is true everywhere—Africa, Asia, South America—that the supreme concern of the foreign missionary must be to help get the local church firmly on its own two feet as quickly, as ruthlessly as is possible: to bring to a rapid end both the appearance and the reality of ecclesiastical colonialism.

I believe it is extremely important to recognise that a certain era of the church's missionary history which began in the early nineteenth century is now coming to its close. It has been closely linked with the colonialist expansion of Europe and the West. Its achievements have been vast. It has greatly, and significantly, altered the geography of christian witness. But it is now almost over. Firstly, because the independent countries of Asia, Africa and even South America are becoming increasingly reluctant to admit pro-fessional missionaries. Secondly, because missionary voca-tions have enormously declined in most countries of Europe and North America. The effect of this decline is already apparent in mission lands and in the next few years it will be even more striking. Thirdly, it would seem that the out-standing intrinsic need, theological and psychological, in all these places is now to stand on their own feet, to become true local churches, self-reliant christian communities. The achievement of this can be enormously impeded by the continued reception of large-scale foreign help, either in personnel or in money.

The world mission of the church goes ever on, but it takes different structural forms in different ages. The pat-tern of the last hundred years, the pattern for which all the modern missionary societies were initially founded, is nearly over; nearly but not quite. Our theme then is—What should the last generation be doing in the few years that remain? How can we ensure that the work of earlier generations of missionaries is not lost amid the tumultuous changes of our era? How can we witness to Christ, the universal Saviour, through the life of the church in the last third of the twentieth century? How can we prepare the way for a new age of mission?

It is historically undeniable that the mission has tended to dominate the new church, even—with the best will in the world—to prevent its really becoming a new church at all; it has tended to keep it a 'mission'. This fact is demonstrable in obvious and in many less obvious ways, in every part of the world from a study of mission history. Thus, it is difficult to believe that for the three hundred years prior to the 1920s in which the churches of India, China, Ceylon and Viet Nam had existed, there was really no single local person fitted to become a bishop. Yet, none was appointed. And when Pius XI requested in the 1920s that names of Chinese priests suitable for promotion to the episcopate be sent to him, the first missionary reply was still that there was no single Chinese priest suitable. I know in our times of an African major seminary in which, not so many years ago, during the canon law course, the section on parish priests was simply omitted with the remark 'None of you will ever be parish priests!' Only the section on curates was to be treated. Such attitudes could only come from a profoundly false general conception of the nature of missionary work and of the proper relationship of the missionary to the local church. Reference to such topics is not a mere matter of historical curiosity. Similar attitudes persist today in many ways and places. A very obvious example is that many missionaries remain highly reluctant (instead of being anxious), to work under a local bishop. Some still maintain that where a majority of priests in a diocese are of a foreign missionary institute, the bishop should be the same. Again, many missionaries are still unwilling to live regularly under a common roof with local co-workers; this is true of both priests and nuns.

But mistaken views of missionary life and commitment may remain at levels far deeper, and ultimately more serious, than those of a conscious 'Yes' or 'No' reply to a particular question. They can remain in a whole complex of attitudes whereby missionaries and missionary societies sometimes try to over-protect themselves and their property from the consequences of the indigenisation of church control. I do not intend to say that it is not necessary to make any terms of agreement at all between missionary society and local diocese or that there is not very often a need to protect individual missionaries. Everyone has his rights, and a foreign priest can be in a particularly helpless position if there is no society to support and defend him on occasion. It is the type of attitude in which such terms of agreement are drawn up which is important.

They can remain in the type of missionary training still provided, which puts the main emphasis on loyalty to an institute and its internal life, rather than on service of a young church; and in which the individual is not really being prepared for immersion within a particular human society and a local church quite other than those to which he has hitherto belonged.

They can remain in the acceptance and enforcement by missionaries of patterns of worship, ministry and church life, inspired by canon law or the religious and pastoral practice of a sending church, which have not been made for (and do not suit) societies very different economically, culturally, educationally.

All this is not to blame past missionaries, above all individuals. In most things they have only too faithfully reflected the church from which they came. It is idle to expect missionaries setting out in the heyday of the post-Vatican I era to have had the ecclesiology, the facility to distinguish essentials from accidentals, the rich mission theory, the understanding of anthropology and sociology, which are becoming possible and indeed necessary today. To analyse the past, both its strength and its weakness, is not to judge. Nor is it surprising if missionaries today are still acting in outdated ways. It is easier to have a new vision than to create new structures, new ways of work.

We do not judge, but we do need to understand. We must understand that both the missionary societies and the young churches largely took their shape at the most rigid, the most neo-scholastic, the most ultramontane, the most centralised half-century in the history of catholicism— that is to say 1870–1920. The churches of Europe too were much influenced by that epoch, but they had also other, older traditions. The young churches and the missionary societies responsible for them took on the character of that age to a very special degree. If the doctrine of Vatican ii in its deepest thrust represents a breakaway from a centralised, uniform, monolithic, view of the church, a view of the Catholic Church as the church of Rome instead of as the churches of the world in full communion with Rome, then it does require from missionaries and from all those working within these young churches a very special response.

Again, as we have seen, it is not only this internal revolution of enrichment and liberation which the Catholic Church is painfully undergoing, but the very rapid change in social and mental conditions taking place in most lands, especially so-called 'mission lands'; the growing gap between rich and poor nations; the total re-shaping of the relationship between the West and the third world, and between the Caucasian race and the other races. All this fantastic complexity of theological, sociological, political, racial, and mental change is crackling around our ears. It all requires a quite radical re-thinking of the dimensions of missionary activity in the church today and of the type of existence proper to those who are called to a special involvement in such activity.

This re-thinking has both its corporate and its individual implications. Let us consider some of them under the headings of personal commitment, training, finance.

I think that in the general course of human history it would be difficult to find a large group of men more totally committed to a cause than have been vast numbers of missionaries. In many parts of the world in the nineteenth century, the average missionary anticipation of life can hardly have been more than two years. For many who did survive, the likelihood of returning home remained slight. Decade after decade, such men and women have gone forth. There are men, old men, whom one has known and buried these last years in Africa who came out around the turn of the century, and have worked there continuously, or almost continuously, for sixty years; Fr LeVeux, for instance arrived in Uganda in 1903. His great work on Luganda vocabulary—over a thousand pages long—was printed in 1917. He was rector of Bukalasa seminary from 1932 to 1947. He died in 1965 and was buried at Bukalasa: sixty-two years after his arrival in the country. We have known such people in many societies and from many countries—men symbolised, perhaps, by Fr Choblet so warmly described in Arthur Grimble's *Pattern of Islands*. Faith and commitment could not be greater, and so it has remained. The hurry with which we have seen old missionaries return to parts of the Congo where dozens of their colleagues had recently been murdered could not make the point more clearly. It is a tradition and an example we must not lose.

The role of people involved in missionary service for a few years has a value of its own, producing a wider cross-fertilisation within the church which can be enriching. But one cannot doubt that the church needs some men, and that God calls some men, to commit themselves to mission for life. Physically the conditions of the old missionaries could be very hard indeed, but the character of the society they had come from, and the mental environment of the contemporary church somehow supported them. Church and western society might quarrel over many things, but almost no one doubted the value of the missionary. Livingstone was everyone's hero. Anti-clericalism, said a French minister, was not for export. It was taken for granted that the missionary's work was for a lifetime, and it was taken for granted too that time was on his side. Progress was believed in, and it was for him. Roughly speaking, the belief was correct. The possibilities of fruitful missionary work were steadily improving in the century 1840–1940. No one could imagine a time when the missionary would not be needed.

Psychologically the missionary's position today is entirely different. The *Zeitgeist* is against him. The 'modern world', unlike the Victorian world, finds little value in him. Most Asian and African governments, though they recognise how much missionaries have done in the past in the educational, medical and social fields and see the need for them today, are trying to whittle the missionary force away, little by little. They look forward to the day—not far off, many believe—when foreign missionaries will be almost redundant.

What sense remains then in the old-time missionary commitment? It seems to me that in present circumstances it is of prime importance to make a really radical distinction between missionary commitment and the organisational–inspirational complex that has grown up following the missionary revival of the early nineteenth century. I have absolutely no doubt that the missionary movement of the last hundred years has been providential, that it has achieved something of the highest importance in salvation history, and that to achieve this it required, roughly, the organisational pattern which it in fact created.

But the work is done, the situation that movement responded to is no more, and much of the machinery it created is today becoming an ever heavier liability. The question now is how to maintain the vigour of the church's missionary function in quite other circumstances. I am sure that the maintenance of that vigour does indeed call for the continued presence of some men with a life commitment to specifically missionary work. But the signs of the times appear to me to be pointing to a far smaller clerical missionary force, and a much less exclusively western one, than we have been accustomed to or made our aim. This force, however, will need a very much more profound training than missionaries have customarily received. The curtailment in numbers must be balanced by—on the one side—a far more active local ministry than has up till now existed in most young churches, and—on the other side—a far wider, effective recognition of missionary responsibility within all ranks of the world church. As a matter of fact, in the last hundred years the truly magnificent effort of the church's missionary army of priests, brothers and sisters has had as its obverse side a very clericalised conception of the missionary task, a lack of missionary commitment (except for the collection of money) on the part of the laity, and a very considerable failure to bring into existence within the missionary field a self-ministering local church community. All these things went together, and now they are changing together. It would certainly be mistaken, and futile, to try and stop the change in one particular element of the pattern: the vocation of the 'clerical' foreign missionary.

The missionary dimension of the church's life must not grow less in the coming years, but the place within it of life-long professionals will surely grow less. It will grow less, but it must not be allowed to fade away. They are needed. But they will be able to respond to today's and tomorrow's needs only in so far as they drastically re-think their role and concentrate on quality very much more than on quantity. They must recognise that the more basic ministries in all local churches have to be done, and can only be done effectively, by members of those churches. The justification of a missionary society must be found in the effective ability of its members to pioneer new fields, to provide specialist services in young churches, and to manifest that quality of felt christian brotherhood which so desperately needs to be manifested between different churches within the one communion, as it needs to be manifested between different tribes and races within the one human family.

But all such tasks require such a specified vocation and such qualitative standards within missionary formation as have—to be honest—hitherto hardly existed. The notion that the training of a missionary priest could consist of the same six years of Noldin and Tanquerey or their equivalents as are taught in any other seminary, plus some conferences on missionary spirituality and the odd lecture from a missionary home on leave—that notion has simply got to go. One is still amazed to see the numbers of excellent men and women bundled out to long term missionary work in a state of blissful ignorance! Men arrive in Africa and are quickly put to work with no previous study of the political and cultural background, no down-to-earth understanding of the way men live in the society they have come to, no adequate course even in language. The long years of training must become years of real cultural growth, of mental adaptation to a new human tradition, of a sustained willingness to learn from 'them' and not only be prepared to give to 'them'.

I think it has to be admitted that there has been a certain rigidity, a lack of cultural imaginativeness, in most nineteenth and twentieth century missionary work—at least until the last few years. The spirit of Ricci, and de Nobili, has on the whole been very notably absent, though it was reborn in the China of thirty years ago in Vincent Lebbe and his disciples, more recently still in the Nigerian centre of Oye Ekiti or again in Bede Griffith's Ashram and doubtless elsewhere. But such initiatives remain too exceptional. We have in fact been tied, at least until the last decade, and even now far more than necessary, by a vast corpus of Roman legislation, on liturgy, marriage, ministry and what have you which has rendered very hollow the theoretical approval of adaptation in the 1659 Instruction of *Propaganda Fide* and in more recent encyclicals. The training given to most missionaries was of an extreme mental rigidity and it is not surprising that as a result the leap of imagination and personal involvement in another society and its own felt needs have too often not been present; yet without these the missionary remains an outsider, a westerner, unable to be leaven in a new dough because he has kept himself strictly at arm's length.

A deep sympathy with the political and social aspirations of the third world; an ability to appreciate such ways of mind and living as the ancestor cult; a theological awareness of the positive place of non-christian religions in the economy of salvation; the stimulating of such things is a central, not a marginal, part in the training of a useful missionary. There are many men in the field today who suffer greatly from the lack of this type of formation.

In the past, time was on our side. The pace of life was slower and the intelligent missionary picked up much as he went along. Today he needs to know more and has less time to learn. Many missionary societies are well aware of this and the combined development of the North London Missionary Institute is a fine example of it. Others still do not appear to be. One thing is absolutely clear to me: that today it is wrong to a person—priest, brother, sister or layman— and wrong to a receiving church and country to send out anyone on long term missionary work unless he possesses a clearly specialised qualification plus a serious general orientation. Even if today an unspecialised person can still be of use, the chances are too great that within a few years he will be out of a job.

Again, the full-time missionary is no longer to be thought of as normally a white-skinned man. On the contrary it is clear that there are more and more parts of the world in which not only pastoral work but specifically missionary work can best be done, or indeed only be done, by the non-white. And perhaps the non-white will operate in quite a different sort of way from the uniformed missionary we have known. We have to be thinking about mission today with China, with Burma, with the Sudan, with Guinea in mind.

Today clerical dress is becoming more and more dispensable, and so is liturgical ornamentation. The priest can be a priest-workman, the married man may already be a preaching baptizing deacon. The liturgy can be wholly in the vernacular. The eucharist can be around the dinner table. All these things revolutionise the possibilities of missionary work in lands closed to the traditional type of missionary activity. At least they do so for men of the same race and of the same standards of living. The missionary of the future may be a travelling salesman like those old Nestorian merchants who carried the christian faith across central Asia in the early middle ages. The contemporary Baptist witness in Soviet Russia is a lesson which we could profitably take to heart. The trappings of our missionary societies can pass, but the missionary function must and will remain.

The amount of money collected in Europe and North America for Catholic missionary projects has steadily grown in the last twenty-five years though it is probable that in a few years it will again decrease. It is true that some of the greatest sources of money, such as *Misereor*, are only prepared to provide it for social, not for ecclesiastical, purposes. But the money raised for the latter—both through the associations linked with *Propaganda fide*, by missionary societies and by bishops and priests from 'mission lands' on their own—has also much increased. The use and abuse of such money presents one of the greatest problems for the missionary church today. It is widely thought that the more money collected the better, that it is bound to serve our true mission in some way. Nothing would seem to me to be further from the truth. The use of money has its own inherent ambiguity. Apart from obvious waste of money— building a vast seminary which then remains two-thirds empty for years, or a magnificent cathedral in a very small up-country town—the intrinsic effects of the use of foreign money on the life of a young church have to be considered.

No one can doubt that foreign missionary personnel, at least in some poorer areas, must have overseas financial support for their personal needs. Again, no one can doubt that richer countries have a grave duty to give economic assistance to poor countries, and rich churches to poor churches. The question is how to implement these principles without undermining the real character of a local church and the ecclesiastical reality of the principles of subsidiarity and self-reliance. The people of God are an earthly, eating, drinking, buying, selling people. It is not only practically advantageous, it is theologically necessary that a local church be itself an economically viable unit. A church which depends for its existence and essential services upon the continuous charity of other churches is not a healthy, properly established church. Basic economic self-reliance is as much part of the establishment of the church, which is the specific purpose of missionary work, as is the indigenisation of its hierarchy. It is something to which we have given too little thought. It is striking today in many places how much more self-reliant Protestant churches in Africa are than Catholic ones; how Catholics easily take it for granted that their church membership somehow entitles them to a regular hand-out from overseas. It is even more striking to see how much money is raised by the independent churches—christians who have completely broken away from any missionary connection. It is of the nature of man that faith and commitment be expressed in economics, and a faith and commitment which are not so expressed are weak indeed.

It is perfectly true that missionaries have stressed the importance of paying church tax in season and out of season, even going as far (too far) as refusing the sacraments (including baptism for their children) to those who fail to pay. The question one has to ask is whether this constant endeavour has not been largely vitiated by the context within which it has operated, especially of recent years. A context in which, first, local christians can see perfectly clearly that missionaries have in fact access to sources of money beyond their wildest dreams; secondly, church institutions have been created and ways of clergy living established which the local church—with the best will in the world—could not support financially. The local christians draw the obvious conclusion: if you choose to erect institutions totally beyond our means, you can provide the financial support yourselves and not look to our meagre resources. It seems to me unreasonable to hope that christians within a diocese will strain themselves to raise money when they see a few miles away a grand cathedral rising with tens of thousands of foreign pounds. Such building poisons the wells, and indeed it poisons the whole growth of a spirit of self-reliance within the local church. Some bishops of wealthy dioceses in America and Europe may today be doing deeper harm with their lavish gifts for some single triumphalistic project, which they can then come out in solemn state to open, than was done by the lack of interest of their predecessors.

The basic principle here as elsewhere is that missionary activity, and its financial aspect, must be deliberately related, not to the possible resources of a missionary society, but to the future health of the local church it is bringing into being. Furthermore, this health will depend on the required budget and institutional pattern of the local church being themselves related to the economy of the society in which it lives. It is impossible to envisage the institutional character and pattern of clerical life of a diocese within a country where the average annual income is £20 in the same sort of terms as those of a diocese where the average income is £500. And yet, practically speaking, that is what we have been doing in many places. It explains why, time and again, the first action of a newly consecrated African bishop is, not to visit the diocese entrusted to him and tackle its pastoral problems, but to pack his bags and take the next plane to the United States. It helps to explain the rather anaemic character of christian life in so many young Catholic churches, which one would expect to be hives of energy; and it provides a striking contrast to the self-reliant, confident attitude to be found among many christians in the Independent churches.

Financial help from abroad too often weakens the young church instead of strengthening it. The missionary in the field has to be constantly aware of this danger. He must constantly ask himself: does this building really contribute to the strength and witness of the people of God here, or is it just an expression of my own inclination to reproduce overseas the institutions I have known at home?

Our central theme is just this: the outstanding missionary requirement of today is the disinterested and imaginative service of the young local churches according to their true needs. A recent letter I received from a missionary in West Africa ended as follows: 'Now alone in a parish of four thousand five hundred baptized and thirty-two outstations with bad communications, I cannot write but do read.' Wherever I go in Eastern Africa I find the same situation: middle-aged missionaries struggling on with ever more christians and fewer priests ... seventeen thousand Catholics in one parish with a single effective priest and he fifty-nine years old; dioceses which have actually fewer priests now than they had four years ago, but twenty per cent more Catholics. That is the situation facing the missionary today, and what is he to do about it? What aid is he to seek? Make an urgent appeal for more missionaries from abroad? Yet no conceivable response could possibly solve our problems, and those problems involve nothing less than the survival of the Catholic communion in many areas. There is, I believe, only one answer, and the whole of the church's future missionary effort should be reviewed in the light of it, and that answer is a drastic adaptation of the pattern of the church's ministry to the inherent needs of church and society in different lands. The function of the missionary must now be to work for that adaptation, and it is only by doing so that he can possibly today fulfil his basic task of 'implanting the church' as the witness to Christ. But that adaptation precisely involves a drastic substitution of indigenous personnel and church structures which are locally viable, for foreign personnel and structures imported from abroad. Of course, such a substitution cannot be done in a day, but it can be started at once, and in many places has been. The missionary's task is to devote his whole mind and energy to it, and to do so effectively means encouraging a way of church life very different from what he has known at home, or can find in the pages of canon law.

Yet, at the same time as the missionary church sets itself anew to recognise the decisive superiority of local self-reliance over foreign spoon feeding (even to the point at times of refusing money and men it might well be able to provide) it has to consider and to do justice to a rather different, but equally pressing, aspect of its mission: social service of a poor society. There can be no possible doubt of the duty of the affluent 'christian' communities of Europe and North America to provide substantial economic help for the underdeveloped world of Asia, South America and Africa. The community of man and the communion of Christ alike require it. There is, of course, no absolute need for that help to be given via professional missionaries. But for a variety of reasons it is often very sensible that it should be, and many missionaries themselves have, anyway, their specialisation and chief personal concern within the field of social service. In many circumstances this aspect of 'mission' must have here and now a true priority, and it may certainly involve the collection and use of large sums of money. Both aspects of mission (the one described more by Vatican II in the *Constitution on the Church in the Modern World*, the other in the *Decree on the Missionary Activity of the Church*) are essential elements in witness to Christ. In theory it is fairly easy to distinguish them, in practice much less so. Indeed some of our most intractable problems arise from the seeming conflict between the call of a self-reliant church on the one hand and that of rapid social development—so often involving the need for large scale expatriate intervention and even direction—on the other. What one must say is that every effort needs to be made to see that the large donations and social help benefit the society as a whole, not just its Catholic section; that the latter is not marked out (as has so often happened) as the privileged beneficiary of extra overseas aid. Moreover, what particular economic help is given to the Catholic community for one reason or another should be such as will not thereby cripple it for the future by making it dependent even for regular 'running costs' on overseas generosity. It is perfectly right that the local church be in part associated with help provided for its own society by overseas churches, but this must not be done at the expense of its own independence or self-respect.

A missionary in the world today is not in an easy situation. The old landmarks fail. The way ahead is far from clear. Maybe this is a gain. It brings out effectively the truly christian character of his life. Perhaps, paradoxically enough, there was something rather too settled, too certain of mind, even too privileged, about the missionary experience of the colonial era. Today the missionary, like every man, must live with his faith. Systems can pass; religious institutes can come and go; but Christ is for always. We believe in him and we believe that christian faith and love and the church which witnesses to him must be spread ever wider. If his faith and calling are strong enough, if he is for Christ in any circumstances, then the missionary of today will not falter. Whether he is to be a tentmaker or a headmaster, a doctor or an agricultural adviser, a travelling salesman or a simple village priest, he will go on—at times feeling 'utterly, unbearably crushed' (2 Cor 1 : 8) and yet not crushed, 'perplexed but not driven to despair' (2 Cor 4 : 8), unsure of the future, but not unsure of God. His grace is sufficient for us, and in that confidence the missionary of today will offer his witness to Jesus of Nazareth, dead and risen, as surely as Joseph Shanahan, as Xavier, as Boniface, as the apostle Paul.

2

THE UNIVERSALITY OF SALVATION

> The church has a single intention: that God's kingdom
> may come, and that the salvation of the whole human
> race may come to pass.
> [Vatican II, *Constitution on the Church in the Modern
> World*, a.45]

In a famous letter written from prison on April 30 1944,
Dietrich Bonhoeffer remarked, 'The Pauline question
whether circumcision is a condition of justification is today,
I consider, the question whether religion is a condition of
salvation.' Bonhoeffer was feeling his way towards a reappraisal, not only of the conditions, but of the content of
'salvation': a reappraisal we are still struggling over. It is
certain that we must find the sense of salvation at least as
much in a corporate reality as in anything individualistic.
'Is it not true to say that individualistic concern for personal
salvation has almost completely left us all?' he asked on
May 5. He even suggested on June 27 that it might be 'a
cardinal error' to regard christianity as 'a religion of salvation' at all. Certainly in subsequent years there has been a
swing of the pendulum from the extremes of individualistic
salvationitis to the other extreme of a (marxist?) collective
salvation, seemingly unrelated to the personal destiny of the
individual human being. But basically the biblical and
Catholic message is, and must be, concerned to do justice
to both—the collective and the personal—and, again, to
salvation as being something within this world as well as
to salvation as being the character of a new age. Bonhoeffer's

own beliefs retained, I am sure, this both-and quality. 'This world must not be prematurely written off,' he wrote again. That surely is the core of his point: salvation is not to be envisaged as a quick way out, an escape route from this world, but it is Christ's guarantee of the ultimate significance, both personal and collective, of human life in the world. It is, moreover, a guarantee that, in the light of the resurrection, transcends, without eliminating, pain and death.

Is christian faith, is religion, a condition for participation in this salvation that Christ guarantees? If it is—recognising the history and present condition of the human race, and what a small part of it has ever been christian—what sense is there to profess that God wishes all men to be saved? If it is not, what sense is there in calling the restrictive history of the old and new covenants the history of salvation? Further, what compulsion is there to evangelise? The continuity of christian faith and doctrine involves the exploration of new questions within a traditional context as also the exploration of old questions in new formulae. Believing that personal salvation is still an essentially meaningful thing but that it can only be properly interpreted within an adequately collective vision, I offer the following thoughts as an approach to how and why the churchless and the religionless share in salvation.

The bible is the record of God's plan for the salvation of man, and it cannot be doubted that, as this plan is fully revealed in Christ, it is a plan without human limitation: God's intention is to encompass the salvation of all men. The initial affirmation that Jesus is the one and only saviour that men can look to:—'There is salvation in no one else. For there is no other name under heaven given among men by which we must be saved' (Acts 4:12),—grows into the fuller realisation that he is the universal saviour, basically as much concerned with the 'many from the east and west' as with 'the sons of the kingdom' (Mt 8:11–12). The early christians became more and more aware of their world-wide

mission (Mk 13:10; Mk 16:15; Mt 28:19; Lk 24:47; Acts
1:8), its universal character, which is its most characteristic
quality, being the consequence of the universality of the
saviour's work. All barriers are down. The gospel must be
preached to all creation, all nations, the ends of the earth,
because Christ died and rose for all men. This universal
extension of Christ's work, clearly present in the synoptic
gospels and Acts, is still more evidently developed in the
fourth gospel. Christ is the light that enlightens every man
(Jn 1:9). St Paul saw this as being absolutely central to his
greatest revelation: 'God has consigned all men to disobedience, that He may have mercy upon all. O the depth
of the riches and wisdom and knowledge of God' (Rm
11:32-3). Or again, the culminating point of that great
chapter 5 of 2 Corinthians: 'For the love of Christ controls
us, because we are convinced that one has died for all;
therefore all have died. And he died for all, that those who
live might live no longer for themselves but for him who for
their sake died and was raised' (2 Cor 5:14-15). Again, 'God
our Saviour desires all men to be saved, and to come to the
knowledge of the truth. For there is one God, and there
is one mediator between God and men, the man Christ
Jesus' (1 Tm 2:3-6). Perhaps it is in Ephesians that the
all-inclusive quality of Christ's work which so gripped St
Paul's thought is best expressed, its first chapter being a
veritable hymn to universality. On the part of God's intention there is surely no limit. All are to be one in Christ
Jesus.

Nevertheless it is clear too from the whole of the New
Testament, that if Christ died for all, once, upon the cross,
the salvation of all is not settled simply like that. There is
an intermediate procedure, whereby the death and resurrection of Jesus are communicated to individuals. The mission of the apostles and the church follows upon Christ's
work, and the work of the mission is to preach that men
may believe, and to baptise. Baptism and faith are the
means whereby men can enter individually into the salva-

tion once achieved collectively. 'Unless a man is born of water and the Spirit he cannot enter the kingdom of God' (Jn 3:5). The response to 'Save yourselves' is to hear the word of the apostles and be baptised (Acts 2:40-1). Those will be saved, Paul says, who call upon the name of the Lord in whom they have learnt to believe, from the preaching of the church (Rm 10:13-17). The church's mission is essentially a work of communication—linking those far off with the once for all event. Thus, in the words of the Council of Trent, 'Though he died for all, not all receive the benefit of his death, but only those to whom the merit of his passion is communicated'. This communication is achieved through faith and baptism. Now baptism is not an isolated event, it is essentially entry into the visible community of those who believe, the life of apostolic teaching and fellowship, the breaking of bread, and prayer (Acts 2:42), which we call the church. Salvation has to be communicated, and the church, in fact, is what we mean by that communication—the community of men who live according to the faith and sacraments of Christ. No individual will share in Christ's salvation unless he shares too in this communication of it to him. And so, if we say there is no salvation outside Christ, we say too that there is no salvation outside the church: *extra Ecclesiam nulla salus*. And this is absolutely clear. Salvation in Christ means sharing in, being a member of, his body, and his body is the church. To share his life, the salvation he came to bring, and not to be a member of his body, the church, would be utterly impossible. But just as he is a visible saviour, so is his church a visible people, entered into by the visible rite of baptism. To deny any of this would be to contradict the clearest witness of the New Testament.

And yet 'he died for all,' and millions are clearly outside this visible church, and through no fault of their own, and the universality of God's intention of salvation is as certain in scripture as the particularity of the means offered for its mediation. Was that intention really to be utterly vitiated by the limitation of the means? Was the 'all' really to come to no more than a few thousand arbitrarily selected from among the millions of humanity? How are we to reconcile the meaningfulness of the universal salvific will of God, the all-powerful, the all-merciful, with the non-universal character of the visible church, the one ark of salvation? And, furthermore, with the possible non-universality of salvation as an ultimate matter of destiny? Here I mean that, though it may be that everyone is finally saved (as Origen held), it is also possible that some are not saved (but how that state of non-salvation is to be envisaged by us, and to what extent it is a state of being at all, is another question). There are, it seems, three stages in the salvific plan of God. There is the initial achievement of it in Christ with its essentially once-for-all character. There is the effective communication of this to men—in an exemplary manner through explicit faith and baptism—and their acceptance of it within a this-worldly existence. There is its ultimate and definitive realisation. We have to reconcile a meaningful universality in God's salvific will, manifested in Christ, with two things relating to the second and third stages: firstly, the seeming particularity of its communication to individuals (dependent upon the limitation of the historical church); secondly, a possible non-universality in the eternal realisation of the plan.

It is clear that christian tradition has stressed much more one side—that salvation is communicated within the visible church; and it has rather neglected to develop meaningfully, though certainly not consistently denying, the other—the concept of salvific universality, and therefore the possibility of salvation beyond the visible limit of the ecclesial communication of salvation. Scripture, we may say, threw its most direct light upon the visible church as the one ark of salvation, and the tendency was to concentrate upon this side of the mystery, as being anyway that which, in the practical order, most concerns church members. Rather little thought was given to the state of those beyond this visible ark, and to God's intention towards them. Yet it is clear, in much Catholic tradition, that the man in the woods, the person who has had no chance of coming into contact with the church, can somehow be saved. If today we speak much more of this, realising the need to develop a theology of God's will with regard to those beyond, this is not then something entirely new, although the extent of it may be new. The root of it has been very much there all the time.

To advance step by step, one may take first the salvation of the Jews before the time of Christ. It is clear that, if Christ is the saviour and there is no other name under heaven given among men by which we must be saved, this did not only become true in the year 33; it was true also of all before that time. All who have been saved are saved in Christ. Faithful Jews before the time of Christ were certainly saved, immediately through faith in their own covenant; but that is not the ultimate principle, for there is only one ultimate principle of salvation and that is Christ; everyone in the Old Testament who was saved, was ultimately justified in the hope of the saviour who was to come. In hope, in desire, and yet for most of them it was not a very conscious or clear desire, for only little by little was a messianic doctrine formulated; certainly we cannot imagine that there was a clear explicit belief in a coming Messiah on the part of all good Jews, but there was in their life an at least implicit hope and desire for the saviour who was to fulfil the whole of the alliance of the people of God. They were not in the messianic community, for it had not yet arrived, but they desired to be. And so from them we get at once this idea of desire. You are not in the church, but you desire to be in. The same is true of a catechumen who dies before he is received into the church. Here it is a very explicit desire; he has not been baptised by water, he has not received the visible communication of salvation, but he desires it. So we arrive at a necessary extension of Jn 3 : 5:

unless a man be born of water, be within the church—or have the desire to be.

The church is the unique visible community of the baptised faithful, and the sacrament of the presence of Christ. But it communicates salvation, not only across clear membership of this sacramental society, but also across the will to it. This was already stated quite clearly by the Council of Trent: people cannot be saved without the laver of regeneration or the desire for it. And St Thomas, talking about the same thing, stated in passing, what has become for me a principle of enormous importance: *Voluntas apud Deum reputatur pro facto* (*Summa Theologica*, III. 68, 2 ad 3—God takes the will for the deed. So now we have a sort of double principle. Clearly, we have first of all the sacramental principle—the sacrament presenting the visible pattern of the redemption. The whole plan of salvation as we know it, the history of salvation that one now talks so much about, is something which was demonstrated and effected in the visible historical order, the sacramental order; the people of Israel, the incarnate Lord, the visible church— here is a sacramental order of things. This is the sign of God's offer of salvation in the world, and is unique in the order of sign, but it does not limit the realm of the thing signified. It is exemplific but not exclusive. We indeed have nothing else to work through, but we must remember that other principle which refers not only to the particular sacraments, but also to that of the church-sacrament itself: God is not bound, as we are, by the sacraments. We who are historically recipients of some part of the explicit revelation of the divine economy, are bound to work in our co-operation with this work of salvation, through the sacramental order of the visible church. But God is not so bound and, beyond those visible frontiers, has others known only to himself, who are not within the sacramental community, but in whom he sees the will and takes it for the deed. The principle of sacramentality is a crucial one; it expresses the visibility of God's action in the world; the church is the sacrament of Christ, Christ is the sacrament of God, as the people of Israel were before him, of God's choice, of God's intervention in the history of the world; but if this principle of sacramentality is a crucial one for understanding redemption, there is this other one which is in a way even more decisive, the principle of voluntariness; both within and without the sacramental order, the ultimate principle is not the visible one, but the acceptance by God of will for deed, salvation through desire.

What is this desire? In the case of a catechumen, we see it as being an explicit, clear desire. For the Jews of the Old Testament, their desire for the Messiah was often much more implicit than explicit, though they had the visible, sacramental attachment to the community which was the precursor of the messianic society. But beyond these there may be a hundred states of varying explicitness, and in some the will to accept by grace what God is offering, the very knowledge of what God is offering, must be very limited indeed. It may not indeed include any conscious knowledge of Christ at all. This was stated very clearly in what the Holy Office wrote to the Archbishop of Boston in August 1949—'God accepts also an implicit desire—so called because it is included in a good disposition of soul, whereby a person wishes his will to be conformed to the will of God', and is thus drawn invisibly into the salvation which comes from Christ alone. Thus, beyond the visible sacrament of the community of the church are the multitudes who are united with Christ, and therefore with the body of the church, by their basic intention and will. God considers the will for the deed and, because of their wills, accepts and sees them as members of the body of Christ. Clearly this will is—in technical theological vocabulary—a supernatural desire, produced in them by the grace of Christ; but at the level of conscious human experience it is a person's honest, generous and sustained response to the religious and ideological obligations, the good causes and human needs he encounters in his given world: above all to the one God that every man encounters in his fellow men.

To how many people does this apply? Now, how many people (or how many christians for that matter) have adequately responded to and finally accepted the grace of Christ offered to them, we cannot begin to know. But we must, I think, hold that it has been adequately offered to everyone; that salvation is universal, not only in its first but also in its second stage; and that if everyone is not in the end a member of the fellowship-body of Christ-saviour, it is each individual's own fault that he is not; and if that decisive fault should not arise in any individual, then the whole body of humanity will be, and must be, members of the finally manifested body of Christ, the heavenly Jerusalem. The communication of the salvation Christ died to bring all men is not then limited to those who can attain it within the visible sacramental pattern. God is indeed committed in historical revelation to not limiting the salvation he has manifested within the historical covenant community to the members of that community.

A key passage here is Romans chapter 5, where Christ is compared with Adam. 'As one man's trespass led to condemnation for all men, so one man's act of righteousness leads to acquittal and life for all men. For as by one man's disobedience many were made sinners, so by one man's obedience many will be made righteous . . . where sin abounded, grace abounded all the more' (Rm 5: 18–20). Grace has reached as far as sin. The influence of the new Adam has reached at least as far as the influence of the first Adam. Now we hold that the state of original sin has affected all men individually except for Jesus and Mary. Therefore it is necessary, if this principle be true, that the grace of Christ must also reach all men individually, otherwise it could not be said that it abounds more than sin. If the influence of Adam's fault really reached every individual, and the influence of Christ's death and resurrection does not do so, then what St Paul says could not be true. But it is true. And therefore, though we cannot know whether at the last trumpet salvation will indeed be universal—that is our third stage—we can and do know that not only were Christ's death and resurrection for all, but they have also been applied to, communicated to, each and every individual. Only thus can we avoid the basic meaningless-ness of saying that Christ died for all, but that many men have been excluded, by no fault of their own, from the effects of the death of the God-man. Only thus can we avoid making of Romans 5 a meaningless mockery. Adam's fault would indeed have abounded far further than the salvific work of Christ. No, if any human being does not enter heaven as Christ died that he should, it is not because that human being is a son of Adam, or any other accidental reason such as that the church never reached him in his locality, but in the end because he, personally, refused to be a brother with Christ. However necessary such a conclusion may be, it presents problems.

What we have to reconcile is the absolute centrality for religious reality of that great sacramental axis going be-tween earth and heaven—Christ, the church, the eucharist, the axis of life, coming down, going up, between God and men—with this effective concern for every single one of the persons he has created, and whose only conceivable destiny is communion with him—a destiny guaranteed, both by the revelation of God's purposeful love in creating personal beings at all, and by the Cross. On the one hand we have the historical incarnational economy of redemption in Israel and the church, this holy history of salvation which, by the very nature of it, includes some people and excludes others. The choosing of the people of Israel involved an exclusion from the plan of God of everybody else. The choosing of the community of the disciples and the apostles, and of the community of the church did the same. The idea of inclusion involves exclusion. What we have to reconcile is this inclusion-exclusion plan of the historical incarna-tional economy of redemption with realisation that, if

God is God, if Christ is Christ, if they are what we believe
them to be, then there cannot be any ultimate barriers imposed by him to communion between him and any single
one of his immortal creatures.

How do we make sense of this dual pattern of salvation?
Of this discovery that after all the traditional preoccupation
with a limited historical community, the subject of the
sacred history of salvation, God really intends the salvation
of everyone after all? One might react: what then does the
church matter? Why is it important to belong to the church,
if, in fact, God considers the will for the deed and gives
grace to everyone, sufficient grace that their will may
embrace salvation? To help us in the doubt and difficulty
that this question does raise, we might appeal to two
principles. First of all, the 'Why' of incarnation. Incarnation is the plan, the pattern which God has adopted for his
revealed dealings with men, for the individual and collective reformation of man in Christ. The point of incarnation
is that the work of God is carried out entirely in accordance
with the principles of human living. Israel, Christ, the
church, represent developing stages of the divine action of
God within the human community. Development is characteristic of human society, itself an intrinsically developing
thing, and if God is going to act with man in man's way, it
must be within a continuous development which is entirely
proportioned to man's natural capacity for growth. What is
God doing? His purpose is to insert the divine communion,
the divine fellowship of Father, Son and Holy Ghost, into
the human order, so that all men can individually come to
share in it. God is not only offering us his friendship, he is
offering it through the natural working of our lives and
across a human fellowship. This is the pattern of the
incarnation, that God enters completely in person into
human society, and thus the axial plan of salvation, as it
slowly dawns upon us, is always within the human way of
life. Now this very fact, that God acts with us according to
our nature, imposes limitations upon God's plan, apparent

limitations. We accept that for Christ; he could only be in one place, he could only speak to a few people, and so on, just because he was man. The principle of the incarnation placed tremendous limitations upon the influence Jesus could have upon men. We take that for granted, but often, rather curiously, we don't accept that the same must be true for the church; yet it is obvious that if the church was going to operate as a human society, which it is, it too has to have the same sort of limitation. Thus it was in the nature of the thing, that the church could not, at least for a very long time, be effectively universal. This isn't just due to the imperfections of christians. If the church was to act as a human society it couldn't be everywhere. To take an extreme case; there were plenty of people in the New World, in America, two thousand years ago, but there was no way the apostles could have got there. If God was going to act through human ways of behaviour, there was an imposed limitation upon the community of the redemption, as well as upon the redeemer. And this was necessary; God had to accept this limitation of the church, which meant the exclusion of some from the visible community, if he was going to make the way of redemption a truly human one. And so there is a necessary evolution in the church, a becoming Catholic, and at least a long period in which, not by anybody's fault but simply because of the nature of the pattern of incarnational redemption, many are excluded. If the church had been able to reach everybody at once, it would not have been acting in a human way at all, it would have been acting in an entirely miraculous way. This could not be if the church was to accept the limitations of space and time implicit in the incarnation and operate humanly, and grow co-naturally with the world it was informing.

It will help us here if we distinguish three planes in the implementation of God's salvific will. Firstly, the most important plane is that of the end, the fullness: the new Jerusalem, the church of Ephesians 1 : 23, the church as she will be when finally all is achieved and fulfilled in Christ, all her qualities fully explicitated; humanity integrally reformed; the bride at last ready for the bridegroom and the wedding feast.

Secondly, there is the plane at any particular stage in the historical process. Still today it does not seem to be God's will that the church should really be everywhere. It remains in the process of *becoming* Catholic. In 100 BC God willed the salvation of the whole world, just as he does in relation to the world of 1970. But he only seemed to be dealing with Israel. Can we imagine that God did not really care about the people outside Israel at that time? Of course he loved them as much. They were his creatures too. But there had to be development within the realisation of the historical plan. Seeing God's will in the history of salvation means seeing something developing, and here you have to consider the will of God according to the stage which the pattern of incarnation, of the historical incarnational establishment of the community of salvation, had reached at that moment. Thus it is clear that it was not part of God's plan that in the apostolic age the church should be established in South America. So, within the history of salvation, God's will must be seen as a developing plan of salvation, whose geography at any given moment is very different from the final fullness which it is mysteriously leading up to. We work towards the end, but it is no necessary condemnation of the church at any given time in history that she lacks the qualitative and quantitative character that rightfully belongs to the end. A programme for 'the evangelisation of the world in this generation' is in one way a constant imperative upon believers but in another way it may be simply an impertinence perpetrated by non-historically minded fundamentalists.

Thirdly, in looking at what we mean by God's will, we find it in its relation to each and every individual. God has a plan for each immortal person he has created, and it is a plan of salvation, even though that individual may be excluded of necessity from the one revealed history of salvation. If you happened to be a Roman in 400 BC, you could not be part of that visible history as it had worked itself out at 400 BC. If you were South American in 600 AD, you could not be in the visible plan of God as it was worked out in your generation. And these are only particularly obvious examples of an enormously very much wider phenomenon. In each case you were excluded from participation in the historical community of salvation in the form it had providentially reached at the moment of your life. But that does not mean that God was somehow uninterested in you individually and had no plan for you. That would be unthinkable. God is love. He knows and loves and is concerned for the salvation of each and everyone. He was not more concerned with the ancient Israelites as individuals than with the ancient Egyptians. As the one passed through the Red Sea and the other drowned, his eternal personal love embraced both. And so, though some people are necessarily excluded from our second idea of the will of God, as it develops within the history of salvation, they will, in fact, be carried into the ultimate fullness of the first and basic idea of God's will, as it is seen at the end. That end is being prepared by all things, but especially, on the one side, by his concern for each and every human being, and on the other, by the historical expression of this concern, through the development of a community of the faithful, which does not limit, but is the sacrament of salvation. If it is like that, one might ask again, why does it really matter if one, individually, is within this particular historical process or not? After all, missionary work is the attempt to draw people, individuals and communities, from the state of affairs, in which they are outside the possibility of sharing in the history of salvation, and bringing them into it. It is not, we see, that you are offering them the possibility of salvation that they did not have before, you are simply bringing them into the history of salvation's explicit community. Now, what is the point of it? The idea that non-church members really were excluded from salvation offered excellent reason for missionary work, but the more we realise the universality of God's love and concern, admit the providential influence of great religions like Islam and Buddhism, and appreciate the real goodness of non-christians, the more puzzled the missionary may become. Why go to all this trouble? Why be a missionary? There is in fact no end of reasons, but here I would consider just one; the necessity of progressive explicitation.

The divine reformation of the whole of human society is being worked out historically in the church. In her the collective human natural evolution, itself part of the plan of providence, is carried up into a supernatural evolution of mankind in the image of Christ. Both at the level of natural sociological evolution, and at that of its continuing supernatural transformation, what is going on is a drawing out from a seed of life of the full-grown tree. Our history is a process of bringing out what was before only implicit in the human condition. Neanderthal man was man as we are, but his human potentialities had not been much developed. The whole meaningful direction of human history and of human living, is a slow bringing out of all that is implicit within us, and making it explicit, the actuation of our individual and collective possibilities. And human life becomes more effectively worth living the more this is done. To help one's fellow men move from a marginal position into a more conscious sharing in the riches of the human condition, is enormously worth while. Now the advance of the sacramental community of salvation involves this same process of explicitation, and extends it into a supremely higher sphere. This work of divine explicitation operates both at the collective and the individual level. And it is always good. The Jews had implicit faith in the Messiah and it was sufficient, but how much better it is if it is made explicit, and you really know Christ Jesus. One may be sufficient, but the other is infinitely superior. The whole, supernatural, christian development of the world follows the natural pattern. The purpose of the task of evangelisation is not to bring to man a sufficient minimum condition for salvation but to witness to the fullness of salvation—of what human life can mean when consciously reformed in Christ. Its effectiveness will necessarily depend upon its here and now quality and must be judged accordingly.

If human history is a process of making explicit the implicit potentialities of humanity, the same is true of all missionary and pastoral work, which operates not only as a force for turning to God, but as one of explicitation at the level of what is highest and most worth while in human life —reformation in Christ. The man in the woods has a sufficient conscious willing of the good to save him, but the spiritual potential in his life has not been developed. How much better that his whole nature, and his living, and his mind and understanding should be transformed by the conscious acceptance of the revelation of God and all that that can mean. The point of the process is to make the spiritual life of man as explicit as possible, so that he can fully, consciously, using all that there is of a man in him, accept the Word of God and the plan of God for him. It is a process in no way confined to becoming a christian, but integral to continuous living as a christian, and to the very collective development of the church, whose character and consciousness of herself grows more explicit through the march of sacred history. Only across such work, of bringing men ever more fully into a meaningful and willed belonging to the historical people of God, can the central reformation of the world in the image of Christ go forward. Across the humanisation of the world by the effort of our continuous action, and the explicitation within the church's lived life of all the seed sown there by the Master, we can come at last to the final state, the definitive will of God, in the New Jerusalem, the city of both earthly and heavenly fullness.

Finally, if we have seen a sort of double pattern of salvation, we know that that is ultimately a phenomenological, not a theological division. There are not two ways; the way inside the church and the way outside the church; all is in Christ who is the one single central axis for God's plans; the axis of Israel, Christ, the Catholic church. Although the historical incarnational pattern which God adopted for bringing redemption to man necessitated the exclusion of some from its visible sacramental dimension, everyone is linked with it in fact at the level of will, and in its end. All who are saved are in Christ, and members of his body. St Paul wrote in Ephesians: 'He has made known to us in all wisdom and insight the mystery of his will. According to his purpose which he set forth in Christ as a plan for the fullness of time to unite all things in him. Things in Heaven and things on earth' (1 : 9–10). This is a hymn of joy in the breaking down of 'the dividing wall of hostility' (2 : 14) which separated Jew and Gentile, in the recognition that God's concern was not confined to the community of Israel. 'Is God the God of Jews only? Is he not the God of Gentiles also? Yes of Gentiles also, since God is one' (Rm 3 : 29–30). God is one. That is the supreme principle, and our hymn of joy today must be in the clearer realisation that God's concern overcomes the frontiers, not only of the old Israel, but also of the new. That if circumcision is not a condition for justification and salvation, no more—in the straight meaning of words—is baptism and church membership. The will of God is to unite all, all things in Christ, all men, both those who are in the conscious community of the redemption, and those who, because of the time or place or culture in which they are living, are excluded from the historical community, but are still, by the love of God, enabled to adhere finally and effectively to the one saviour in his one body.

THE THEOLOGY OF SOCIAL DEVELOPMENT WORK

Both the Pastoral Constitution of Vatican II, *The Church in the Modern World*, and Pope Paul's encyclical *Populorum Progressio* have called Catholics most emphatically to take part in the work of social development. This is, of course, nothing really new. It is a continuation of the Catholic tradition of systematic concern with the 'corporal works of mercy' within a modern context. A very large part of missionary work, especially as it has been carried on since the nineteenth century, has had as its immediate purpose the secular improvement—in health and education—of the people whom missionaries approached. The striking development of missionary medical orders is an obvious example of this. For christian missionary work, in general, it would be strikingly untrue to say that there has been a concern for men's souls but not for their bodies.

The urgency of the situation today, as the gap between rich and poor nations grows still wider, and the objective inadequacy of what has been done hitherto (which modern information services can show so clearly) are the reasons for a greatly increased insistence upon the priority of this work within the total context of christian living. It is not a special call for the few, it is in a very real way the central duty of the whole church in today's world. Seen with such full dimensions, as impinging upon the conscience of christian communities everywhere, this call to social development work is indeed something new.

That christians must be concerned with the material needs of their neighbour is obvious enough. Parable after parable stresses it. The final judgment, as described in Matthew 25:31–46, is visualised as wholly dependent upon service or negligence of those in need. Nevertheless in much christian thinking it remains far from clear exactly how such work, and participation in general in the 'secular' round—in the political, economic, cultural field—is related to 'religion' and to the proclamation of that message of 'salvation' to which the Church is above all committed.

Earthly progress must be carefully distinguished from the growth of Christ's kingdom. Nevertheless, to the extent that the former can contribute to the better ordering of human society, it is of vital concern to the kingdom of God.

[*The Church in the Modern World*, 39]

In what way is that 'vital concern' to be understood?

Are those 'good works' whose immediate purpose is secular improvement just a sort of way whereby the christian may fill up his time when not in prayer and so demonstrate himself as somehow fit for salvation? What is the value of the works in themselves, and is that value-in-itself one only in the secular field or necessarily also in the religious field? If salvation is full deliverance in and through Christ from sin and all that goes with sin, what intrinsic relationship has it with deliverance from dirt, from hunger and malnutrition, from ignorance, from disease, from the moral humiliation of being a political nobody, from patterns of living controlled by these things which instil into man a constant crippling fear? Social development work is the deliberate, consistent activity to deliver man from such a state: how is it related to the gospel of deliverance in Christ?

A first answer might be that it is not related at all, and it is an answer that has often been given. The gospel refers to a deliverance provided in 'the next world' and that deliverance will be all the surer the more you have accepted the lack of a secular deliverance in this one. In the words of the Emperor Napoleon:

> What is it that makes the poor man take it for granted that ten chimneys smoke in my palace while he dies of cold—that I have ten changes of raiment in my wardrobe while he is naked—that on my table at each meal there is enough to sustain a family for a week? It is religion which says to him that in another life I shall be his equal, indeed that he has a better chance of being happy there than I have.[1]

The deliverance of the gospel has here become, as a reality purely of the next world, a substitute for deliverance on earth. This is the 'pie in the sky' view, a sugar candy mountain, but it has little to do with the real gospel, which says much more about an over-turning of situations in this world than about the condition of things after death.

However, even christians who would repudiate Napoleon's viewpoint as a caricature of the truth still often both think and act as if the two types of deliverance remain basically unrelated, separate parallel pursuits. One is 'secular', the other 'religious'. The one brings about the common good of temporal society, the other leads to salvation. Man is a citizen of two societies and has obligations in both of them. If you neglected your duties as an earthly citizen, you would certainly not be a thoroughly good christian, and yet the duties themselves have often seemed intrinsically unrelated to one another. The traditional Catholic philosophy of 'two perfect societies' tended to encourage this attitude.

A basic difficulty with this view was to discover what religious duties one really has, if they are distinct from one's temporal duties. The New Testament, in fact, is full of commands of temporal service, of avoiding any trace of a

[1] Quoted in A. Vidler, *The Church in an Age of Revolution*, London (Penguin Books) 1961, 19.

Dives-Lazarus division, of responding in short to 'the message which we have heard from the beginning' which is 'that we should love one another' (1 Jn 3 : 11). And this love is always understood as being one only clearly identifiable in terms of this material world: 'If anyone has the world's goods and sees his brother in need, yet closes his heart against him, how does God's love abide in him?' (1 Jn 3 : 17). The proof of the presence of the gospel's deliverance from the very beginning was one of deliverance from material pressures: 'the blind receive their sight, and the lame walk, lepers are cleansed and the deaf hear' (Mt 11 : 5). The proof that the gospel is finally accepted by any man is of the same type—that he has himself participated in the work of temporal deliverance: 'I was hungry and you gave me food' (Mt 25 : 35).

It is clear that right from the beginning the christian gospel of 'religious' deliverance was in its content simply not separable from the field of temporal deliverance. The new paschal mystery cannot be divorced from its context— the Exodus deliverance, which from being a particular event had come to express the permanent pattern of God's action on his people: 'I have seen the affliction of my people . . . have heard their cry because of their taskmasters . . . and I have come to deliver them' (Ex 3 : 7–8). And so 'Yahweh saved Israel that day from the hands of the Egyptians' (Ex 13 : 30). The biblical concept of salvation was one of God's delivering his people from temporal pressures. He frees them from the tyranny of Egypt, he gives them a land where they can be free and properly fed. He guards them from the attacks of aggressive neighbours. All the imagery of salvation—tower and walls and rock—with which we are so familiar, derives from an absolutely concrete context: only a strong fortress on a rock could 'save' one from raiding Philistines or Babylonians.[2] Any post-temporal salvation that God offered was entirely 'put across'

[2] See T. Paul Verghese, *Salvation: the Meaning of a Biblical Word*, International Review of Missions, October 1968, 399–416.

to his people in terms of deliverance from the immediate overwhelming fear and need, whether it be of the people as a whole or—more and more, later on—of the individual pressed upon by society, hard circumstances or agony of spirit. Salvation, the deliverance which God brings, always starts with, and is found within, deliverance from here and now secular pressures.

What was true of the Old Testament remains true of the New. In each of them is denounced any attempt to establish a separate religious field ('the temple, the temple, the temple'; 'Lord, Lord') which could have validity apart from involvement within the work of secular deliverance. The deliverance brought by the new paschal lamb includes and fulfils all that was offered in the Israelitic theme of redemption of which Exodus was the prototype. The christian gospel of redemption was manifested from the very beginning in a pattern of predominantly this-worldly deliverance: from the slavery of being deaf, dumb, blind and paralytic. Living christian faith is necessarily a commitment to see 'religion' in terms of participating in here and now relief: 'Pure religion is this: to visit orphans and widows in their affliction' (Jas 1 : 27).

The work of secular redemption can in no way then be regarded as in itself irrelevant to or distinct from that of religious redemption. The latter can, quite literally, have no sense without the former. But what is their exact relationship? To say that one is simply preparatory to the other would seem quite inadequate because, in fact, it provides its continual and finally decisive reference. Nor does it seem very satisfactory to say that one forms 'part' of the other. How big a part? And how do you balance the claims of one part against the other? Yet to identify the two is equally dangerous. It makes the temporal and the limited into the ultimate. Temporal redemption is redemption from a mass of constantly changing things, one replacing another. If it is not foreign domination, it is economic injustice within the community, the tyranny of a husband, boredom. The great danger, and a true idolatry, is to make of any particular one the ultimate deliverance. Indeed the greatest deliverance possible in this world is exactly to come to realise both the limited evil that any pressure upon one finally is, and the limited good that its removal will bring: not to make of any secular tyranny the ultimate evil nor of any secular reform the ultimate good.

I think that a passage from Paul Tillich can help us here:

> There are three possible relations of the preliminary concerns to that which concerns us ultimately. The first is mutual indifference, the second is a relation in which a preliminary concern is elevated to ultimacy, and the third is one in which a preliminary concern becomes the vehicle of the ultimate concern without claiming ultimacy for itself. The first relation is predominant in ordinary life with its oscillation between conditional, partial, finite situations and experiences and moments when the question of the ultimate meaning of existence takes hold of us. Such a division, however, contradicts the unconditional, total, and infinite character of the religious concern.... The second relation is idolatrous in its very nature. Idolatry is the elevation of a preliminary concern to ultimacy.... The third relation between the ultimate concern and the preliminary concerns makes the latter bearers and vehicles of the former. That which is a finite concern is not elevated to infinite significance, nor is it put beside the infinite, but in and through it the infinite becomes real. Nothing is excluded from this function. In and through every preliminary concern the ultimate concern can actualise itself.
>
> [*Systematic Theology*, I London 1953, p. 15–16]

Secular redemption, it seems to me, is 'the bearer and vehicle' of religious redemption; only through it can the latter here and now 'actualise' itself, though—as the possibilities of secular redemption are many and varied—it may actualise itself in many different ways. To say it in another way: one is the sacrament of the other. Secular deliverance provides 'matter' for which the gospel gives the interpretative norm. The latter takes the temporal need of men—escape from Egypt, from leprosy, from poverty and ignorance, from racial tyranny—and through it reveals a deliverance which goes far beyond the immediate need. But this ultimate deliverance cannot, in a world of space and time, meaningfully actualise itself except sacramentally across immediate deliverances. Hence it is the prime duty of the bearer of the message of ultimate deliverance to provide it with an adequate vehicle of secular significance. Secular liberation is finally falsified if its perspective is not thus carried up beyond itself, while religious liberation becomes a bogus message (opium of the people) if it is not here and now actualised in terms of temporal redemption.

Just as the church is the sacrament of God, and the sacramental matter of God's love is love of man, the sacramental matter of christian liberation is liberation from the material and psychological pressures of the world, and the sacramental matter of communion with God is communion with men. In each case one here and now points towards, embodies, makes actualisation of possible, but does not exhaust the dimensions of, the other.

To preach about christian deliverance without 'incarnating' it in any immediate liberation—social, psychological, or economic—would be like preaching about the eucharist but never actually celebrating it. The religion of the incarnate Lord requires that, just as the ultimate word only comes to men across limited human words fully partaking in the historicity of this world, so ultimate redemption comes to us and makes sense across limited redemptions fully partaking of the materiality and historicity of temporal life. To preach redemption otherwise is not to preach the redemption of the incarnate Word.

None of this is new in itself. Secular concern has always been the mark of the true christian, and in every age saints and prophets have called the church away from ecclesiasticism and back to serving the world as being not an extra but the very core of gospel living. Quite rightly—this being a very condition of continuing effective work in this world— response to the call has been institutionalised. Without systems and institutions man's needs just cannot be regularly met. Yet how often, with the course of years, the very thrust of a work slowly changes. An institute founded to serve the poor develops into another comfortable case of care by the haves for the haves. To how many religious institutes and monasteries has this happened, and it is then justified by the need for obtaining sufficient money to maintain themselves and their stately buildings.

The only answer to this is renewal in every age, new thrusts outwards and a leaving of now dead branches to fall from the tree. What is new to this age is our greater knowledge and technical possibilities. Rapid methods of communication, tinned foods and dried food, the whole apparatus of modern living and modern food production enable one to implement the epistle of James and the parable of the Good Samaritan on an inter-territorial and inter-continental scale hitherto unimaginable. Modern invention enables one, and therefore obliges one, to find one's neighbour, the man in need on the road to Jericho, not only in the same street, but anywhere on the same planet. And our present-day knowledge shows us so much better what the deeper needs are.

Just as 'Go ye and teach all nations' remains the same command for each century, but its implementation now must be done in quite new ways, so 'if a brother or sister is ill-clad and in lack of daily food' is the same message today as yesterday, but the scope of its possible—and therefore requisite—application has been completely overturned by these modern possibilities. These, infinitely more than past resources, enable us if we will, not merely to feed the hungry from day to day but to give them far more adequate means to feed themselves, to so reshape the environment that they need be hungry no more. We can see better too that man must be freed, not only from poverty and hunger, but from the social humiliation that goes with them; that this is not achieved by simply handing out emergency rations, but can be brought about by the deeper work of helping men to help themselves which builds up the sense of personal dignity in self-reliance, and is recognition of man as man and not just as mouth. Again, we see today, as we could not before, how much poverty and social humiliation are the products of corrupt political and economic systems; how effective christian charity has, therefore, to work at changing the system—whether it be the political disqualification of non-whites in South Africa or international terms of trade—rather than at continuous alleviation of the lot of the worst sufferers within the system.

Modern techniques, in fact, which have transformed 'charity' both into political action and into 'development work', really permit a deeper expression of charity, because they can respond to wider and more lasting needs of man than could the old ways. I was hungry and you fed me, but also I was humiliated and you helped me to the dignity of self-reliance, to being a first class citizen. As the root cause of conflict, bitterness and war in the world is, more than anything else, unfair economic conditions, the gap between the affluent and the poor, the real control of power by privileged minorities, and the attitudes of greedy attachment and envious seeking which such conditions produce in men and groups of men, so the only effective way of peace-making is in the last resort to remove such gaps. Development work and political action—in certain circumstances even revolutionary action—are truly a direct response to the call of Matthew 5:9, 'Blessed are the peacemakers.' Hence Pope Paul can call 'development' the new name for 'peace'.[3]

Not only the church but all that is most alive in human society is today becoming aware of this overwhelming need

[3] *Populorum Progressio*, no. 87, cf. 76–9.

for social development in so many parts of the world. The implications of being man with men require of the affluent that they express with a quite new determination and in hard material terms the reality of human brotherhood. The Pearson Commission, sponsored by the World Bank, has called for the wealthy countries to contribute annually at least one per cent of their gross national product to overseas aid. For most countries, notably Britain, this would mean a considerable increase on what is given at present. In fact the opposite is happening. Overseas aid is steadily diminishing: in Britain during the last few years of Labour government from 0·53 to 0·39 per cent of the gross national product. Yet Britain has a particular obligation to give overseas aid for no other country has profited comparably from the spoils of overseas rule. Christians in the affluent societies who put their own increased standard of living as the primary political objective in place of that of service to the needy either at home or in the under-developed world are betraying the central implications of their gospel faith.

The church as an institution has also the duty in many circumstances to commit itself directly to development work. Where this is being undertaken adequately by other agencies, notably government, it is for the church to co-operate chiefly at a personal level; but where governments and other organisations are not doing this sufficiently—for instance, neglecting certain areas or strata of the population —the church must not be frightened of directly undertaking development projects, and this may still often be needed in Africa. Such projects will inevitably be on a far smaller scale than governmental ones, they should be undertaken ecumenically wherever possible, and they do of course require full technical expertise. Success can seldom be achieved without the good will of government, and a pattern of overall supervision by the government but immediate stimulation and management by the church may often be the most suitable one.

The gospel of salvation proclaims a God who led our

fathers out of Egypt, freed them from their slave-drivers, and his salvation must still be seen and experienced across some modern exodus, deliverance from the secular bonds which ever bind his people. And if the church is the sign of salvation, of the sort of salvation which the bible proclaims, she too is necessarily a vehicle of secular as well as religious deliverance. Her mission is at once preaching the word (kerygma) and temporal service (diakonia), two things which in fact only make sense together. They can be considered as constituting the 'form' and 'matter' of the sacrament which the church is. *Kerygma* is the message, an interpretation, essentially ineffective when it has nothing to interpret. The matter for interpretation is the church's *diakonia*—service, development, secular liberation. Together, and only together, do they constitute the sacrament of salvation.

4

PERSONAL FAITH AND SOCIAL
INVOLVEMENT

What are the personal implications of the christian gospel in
the socio-moral field? If, as we have seen, it is of the nature
of the church to be at once a *kerygma* embodied in a
diakonia: a message of divine liberation actualised in terms
of temporal liberation, then the christian by the very fact
of being a christian has basic obligations not only towards
the Word of God but also towards the service of the worldly
community. The original Exodus message of divine liberation became at once a programme of human action: the
statement that God would free his people was followed immediately by a command: 'I send you' (Ex 3 : 10). We cannot opt out of this sending. The christian is caught up by
his faith in the necessity of manifesting God's redemption,
of being each in his own individual way a credible combination of *kerygma* and *diakonia*.

What has the gospel message to tell us about the christian's basic attitudes to human society? I think it is possible
to answer that question under the headings of incarnation,
commitment, solidarity, judgment and revolution. These
are not to be taken in isolation, each involves the others and
would have little meaning apart from the rest; nor, of
course, are they exhaustive.

The fact of the incarnation is foundational for the
christian approach to life. It may be true of some religions
that they present a specifically spiritual doctrine, a way of
escape from the material world, but this can in no way be
the sense of christianity. Christianity is not an escape from

the world, it is not a spiritual doctrine that matter does not matter; on the contrary, the take-off point of christianity is exactly a plunging into the physical and the material. The Word of God became flesh. What is highest and first in our concept of the real became flesh, was identified with the material, and entered the human community on a level of equality. The Word became flesh to dwell among us, full of grace and truth. And we saw him. God was in this physical, material world, and by sharing such a life proved its value. Only in this context can we make any sense of christianity; of a religion which does not find its source in a belief that material things are bad, irrelevant or to be ignored, but in a belief that God in some way identified himself with the material, entering into human society not only at the level of spirit but at the level of flesh.

This is basic. Unless we take the incarnation seriously, we cannot begin to imagine what the proper approach of a christian will be to the problems of a society in which he lives. All the way through this is so. Take the very nature of the church; to be exact, it is an eating and drinking society. How did the apostles try to define themselves when questioned? 'We are the people who ate and drank with Jesus of Nazareth.' The very heart and centre of christian living is not a 'spiritual' thing at all, it is a meal, a consecrational meal. And we are consecrating all the way through. Christianity is a consecration in faith of material things, of earthly life, of the full acceptance and recognition of physical, biological living. Christ took the sharing of men together in a meal with a common loaf, which is broken and eaten, with a common cup which is drunk. It is from this that the meaning of the church is drawn. Material things utterly consecrated: The church, a group of people significantly united at this grossly material level. Eat, drink, these words provide the core of Jesus' final and most characteristic commandment. Eat this, drink this in remembrance of me.

We need to take that very seriously because there always

is a danger of a false christianity which engenders shame for the body, and which suggests that christianity is somehow a getting away from the physical whereas on the contrary the very heart of church life is to be found in something which is physical; and it is through participation in the physical that we are renewed in the spirit. We have to participate because God himself participated. He chose to participate in our total way of life and type of society; he had made man in this sort of a society, and he redeemed us through it and in it. Redemption is no escape from it. Our belief is that Christ rose from the dead in the flesh. As we proclaim in the Apostles' Creed, our hope is in the resurrection of the body. Now there is little sense in believing in the resurrection of bodies unless we value bodies and work to see that people's bodies are going to be worth raising again. This is the very heart of our belief: Christ died in the flesh and rose in the flesh and we have to live in the flesh, finding salvation through the whole processes of an earthly society which make sense only in terms of man as a fleshly reality. It is in the flesh that we find the spirit, and the triumph of the spirit does not come through liberation from the flesh, but through their mutual transformation.

To turn to the theme of commitment. By this I mean total personal adherence to a cause or to a person, the giving of yourself without reserve to that in which you believe. This is quite central to christianity and always has been: we have a faith and a vocation and we accept them completely. A christian gives himself totally. Christ did not say, 'Come along on Sunday for an hour or two'; he said, 'Sell all you have, drop everything, follow me.' No one who looks back is fit for the kingdom of God. In Christ we are aware of an absoluteness of demand placed upon the individual—a demand which was very shocking then and is still very shocking now, coming as it did from the voice of a man, one like ourselves, a carpenter's son. In teaching his first disciples Christ gave a pattern and a model, not only of doctrine but of the way of acceptance of his doctrine which was to be normative for all future generations of believers. And in this norm total commitment is of the essence. There is no room for a half-and-half attachment: follow me. He that is not with me is against me. If you are going to accept this at all, then accept it totally. Christ's call is a command that is to be followed in every moment of our lives, in the totality of our work, employment, thinking, love-making. It is a call for a radical departure from old things and an unlimited commitment to the newness of following him. That is faith.

'Leave all' is an absolute command. It is also a metaphor. It included work, houses, lunch and supper, clothes, as well as wives and family. Only Francis of Assisi walking off naked in the market place fulfilled it completely, and he only in the order of sign. Leave all and keep all. The apostles were later back at their nets and not faithless to their calling because of it. Paul maintained his employment as a tentmaker. Essentially 'leave all' is neither a commandment to absolute poverty nor to selective sacrifices but to a radical subordination of things to people and of people to God—but to a God who is found in people. That is what christian commitment signifies.

To play with Christ, to make of this following an external profession but not a real on-going commitment of soul and body, is indeed to play with fire. What in truth does Christ involve for the christian? He told us that a disciple is not greater than his master. He is perfect if he is as his master is. Following means following, means doing the same. 'I come not to be served but to serve.' Greater love than this no man can have than he lay down his life for his friends, for other men. When we see what Christ is, we see that he is the person completely given to others, to the community, to serving people. Only in the light of what Christ is and does can the disciple's commitment to him, to doing the same as he did, be interpreted. Commitment to Christ means commitment to service. Following him means a total commitment of the disciple to the community because that is exactly what Christ himself was: totally at the service of others. I came not to be served, but to serve. Follow me. The extent of service required of the disciple is the extent of service provided by the Master.

Evidently this leads us on to our third theme, which is that of solidarity, of the christian having necessarily to serve the fellowship of the human community. Take first of all the famous lines in Matthew which describe how a lawyer asked him which is the great commandment in the law and Jesus replied: 'You shall love the Lord your God with all your heart and with all your soul, and with all your mind. And a second is like it: You shall love your neighbour as yourself.' Very good, but Jesus was here quoting the Old Testament; in his own teaching and that of the early christians the two commandments cannot be so clearly differentiated. It can indeed be misleading to say that there are two commandments at all, as if one might then be fulfilled without the other whereas for the Master the only sure proof and expression of the first is necessarily the living of the second. In the end the only test offered in Matthew 25 for the love of God, being blessed of the Father, is the love and service of others: If you love those in need and help them sincerely then you do indeed serve Christ and love God. St John tells us the same. 'If anyone says "I love God", and hates his brother, he is a liar; for he who does not love his brother whom he has seen, cannot love God whom he has not seen. And this commandment we have from him that he who loves God should love his brother also' (Jn 4: 20–21). It is absolutely involved in the nature of loving God as a christian sees it that he loves other people and works for others. John explained it further when he said: 'If anyone has the world's goods and sees his brother in need, yet closes his heart against him, how does God's love abide in him? Little children, let us not love in word or speech, but in deed and in truth' (1 Jn 3: 17–18).

If a man is economically well established and sees others in need yet refuses to share his affluence effectively with them, it is impossible that he be a christian. He may be a priest or a member of a religious order, but he is not a christian. How many people are christians in word, in speech, in name, but not in deed and in truth, because they are not doing exactly what is essentially required to be a christian: if you are to love God you have to be one with your neighbour and to show it materially in the facts of economics. You cannot love God whom you have not seen, if you are not loving and serving and therefore sharing your goods with someone who is in need and whom you do see. Somebody asked Jesus 'who is my neighbour?' and Jesus gave his answer in terms of the Samaritan: Your neighbour is the man you may never have met before, but he is near and he needs help. The bishop passed and he did not stop, and the priest passed and he did not stop, and then a religious nobody came along and he did stop. Jesus was pointing out how easily the most involved representatives of institutional religion can cease to live by the spirit of God, and how in the concrete existential situation it may be someone quite different who really represents the mind of God, who recognises his neighbour and the unalterable exigencies of human solidarity, and shares his goods with him. The words of Christ are extremely radical but many of them are so familiar to us that we really don't take them very seriously. We think they are just beautiful little stories, but they aren't. They are fiercely exigent and Christ meant them to be so.

The human solidarity Christ calls us to is clearly not one of conformity with the spirit of the times, of accommodation, but one that issues in judgment. 'Even now the axe is laid to the roots of the trees' (Lk 3:9). Repent. The various establishments of Jesus' time—Sadducees, Pharisees, scribes—all alike come under fire. The worldliness of incarnational commitment has to be very unworldly indeed. Ultimately, not Constantinian, not baroque, not clerical, but Golgotha-like. The christian commitment to the world is so intense that the world itself cannot bear it and there is mutual judgment. I tell you solemnly, go away from me. Crucify him. Outside the city's gate.

It is an essential part of the collective moral witness of christians to manifest the judgment of Christ upon society, upon the whole of society, the Left as the Right, Hanoi as well as Saigon, upon Washington and upon Moscow. In doing so, one has still to exercise discrimination. Christ is kinder to the publican than the Pharisee. There are sins of weakness but there are sins too crying out to heaven for vengeance. True christian commitment does involve taking sides, even in a world where no side is ever wholly right, with all the risks and partialities this cannot but involve, and it does include action: to show mercy as the Samaritan traveller showed mercy—this can mean not only bandaging the wounds of those already bullied, but also shielding the weak while the bully is still present. This holds as true for the group—for the victimised minority (or majority)— as it does for the individual.

Such a radical commitment of the christian in solidarity with his brothers, compelled by faith to participate in God's own judgment upon the times—the times of which one too is part—, involves revolution and nothing less; there is a vision of this opening all the way through the New Testament, from the Magnificat on. 'He has put down the mighty, he has raised up the lowly, he has filled the hungry, he has sent the rich away empty.' The words are magnificent. What could be stronger? As God works through secondary causes, the implication here is no less than the divine countenancing of social revolution. The Gospel cries out for a reversal of accepted society of a most drastic and radical kind. It was required 2,000 years ago and it is required today; and that means too a reversal of our thoroughly bourgeois, middle-class standards of behaviour. It is true that many social revolutions have come to nothing more than the usurpation by a new minority group of the old privileges and the old way of judging, but that is not the revolution of the gospel.

If a man with gold rings and in fine clothing comes into your assembly, and a poor man in shabby clothing also comes in, and you pay attention to the one who wears the fine clothing, and say, 'Have a seat here, please,' while you say to the poor man, 'Stand here...' have you not made distinctions among yourselves...? But if you show partiality, you commit sin.

[Jas 2 : 2-4, 9]

One cannot be much more severe than that. If you see someone drive up in a Benz to your front door and therefore you are polite, you bring him in and give him a drink, and someone else comes along in dirty clothes asking for a shilling and you shut the door on him, you have shown partiality. You have identified yourself with the standards of the world and you have denied Christ. Terrible words; for are not we, most of us, doing just this so much of the time? Yet this is the nature of christianity, and there is no other. There is a sort of sociological catholicism, a comfortable identification with the institution, but there is no other christianity. Christ calls for a real revolution in our personal and collective standards of behaviour, in our judgment on society, in our sense of what is fitting and what is intolerable, in our vision of what must be done. It is not surprising that we have these words: Children, how hard it is to enter the Kingdom of Heaven. It involves a painful revolution in our mental attitudes and a painful revolution in our society. Painful because it goes utterly against the grain of every establishment. How hard it is! 'Blessed are you poor! Woe to you that are rich! Woe to you that are full now!' What a realisation we find in the gospels of the corrupting effect and the disastrous human consequences of great wealth when it is possessed in a society where there are wide differences of wealth. It is in parable after parable: the judgment on the Dives-Lazarus situation. Christ required of his disciples a really radical reversal of human standards and a revolutionary upsetting

3

of the capitalist money-centred approach to life. You can
not serve God and money and most capitalist-grounded
establishment society serves money. Everything else becomes
the expression of a status measurable in money power.
That modern society is centred upon Mammon and not
upon God is basically and at its best the marxist critique
of it but it is also the christian critique, the judgment of the
Gospel. 'A man's life does not consist in building up a
superfluity of possessions,' and we must be convinced that
as christians we are not working to obtain the highest possible per capita income in the world. We are working to
make of human society a kingdom of justice, a world where
the Dives-Lazarus situation has ceased to exist, where instead each gives according to his capacity; each receives
according to his need.

I have tried to illustrate from the New Testament the
only possible spirit with which to approach the problems of
society. A christian vocation involves total commitment, a
commitment to the seeking of Christ who is identical with
the world in need, it involves the human solidarity which
is at once service of others and a sharing in community; it
involves recognising that the world as it is today, or as it
was in the time of Christ or at any intervening time, is so
falsely shaped that it calls for radical dissociation and a
revolutionary change. When we ask what kind of revolution, we are putting a further question, but let us remember
that the evils to be done away with are within the visible
world; they cannot be tackled only at the level of spirit.
Action must be in the flesh. Let us remember too that
radical reform cannot but have some appearance of violence,
if only because it has necessarily to overcome the opposed
will of many vested interests. It is hard not to hold that
many of the violent revolutions of history were, in christian
judgment, right and proper. It is hard also not to hold that
the situation today in such countries as South Africa and
Rhodesia is so intolerably unjust as to justify violent revolution, and it is a revolution which in one way or another

concerns us all, for the world is today in the last analysis a single political and moral society.

No man can comfortably identify himself with the justice of God. Nothing is more dangerous than to see the sword of man as the sword of divine justice. And yet, dangerous things cannot be wholly set aside. It is God himself who has revealed to us some ways of his judgment. This judgment is outside of and over every one of us; yet at the same time we are somehow obliged to concretise it ethically in our own actions, inadequate as such concretisation must always be. Man cannot do other than attempt to embody the condemning judgment of God in revolutionary action just as he attempts to embody the enjoining judgment of God in his laws.

We are called to a total change of heart, to a 'metanoia' of renewal. But because we are social beings and political beings and economic beings, our metanoia has to be social, political, economic. It involves every dimension of being man, a man among men. Even now the axe is laid to the roots of the tree. Never in human history has there been more flagrant wealth, never a wider and more evident division between rich and poor, never more war, more obvious domination of the world by and for the affluent. In these circumstances christian faith demands total involvement in the mission to change. A christian cannot stand apart and say: 'I will live my little spiritual life here by myself in my comfortable house.' That is not being a christian. Being a christian means having heard the call to follow the man who both lived and died for others and being committed to the service of a revolutionary change to establish a world in which there is no napalm, no Auschwitz, no scores of children abandoned in the gutters of Calcutta, no 'whites only', no Dives and Lazarus.

Perhaps that is an eschatological dream, but if christian belief looks to a New Jerusalem of the future in a way that to the unbeliever may seem simply dream-like, it also accepts and makes real an eschatology realised here and now. The message of Christ for the city of men presses on us in the immediate present and, hard as it is, it is for the true disciple first valiantly to accept and then, in both fear and hope, to apply.

5

THE MORAL CHOICE OF VIOLENT REVOLUTION

The world today is a place of revolution. This may not be new but it is significant. The social, political and economic condition of the mass of the population is so unjust in most of South America, southern Africa and elsewhere that very many despair of peaceful, 'constitutional', remedies and turn to violent revolution as the only conceivable way of responding to and changing the 'institutional violence' of government.[1] Christians are being torn apart by the dilemma with which this confronts them. For years christian thought has been growing increasingly pacifist, increasingly impatient with the 'just war' theology whereby christians on each side in every war were enabled to justify their belligerence. On one side today the call is to a really telling witness to the love which needs to be credibly manifested in a violent world by the renunciation of violence, in line with the christian church of the first centuries, with Tolstoi, Gandhi, Martin Luther King. On the other side is the call to an equally self-denying witness to the love of neighbour which can only be credibly manifested in a very unjust world by taking up the burdens of the oppressed, sharing in their struggle, fighting, suffering, dying with them.

[1] To speak in particular of the tyranny in these parts of the world does not mean that one thinks it necessarily worse than that in Russia, Czechoslovakia and elsewhere, but it does seem more open to effective action on the part of christians; it is, secondly, a tyranny often maintained by professed christians and, thirdly, it is one to which the main christian body has been far less opposed than to that of communist countries.

Which is the truly christian way?

Christianity is revolutionary but it calls primarily to a revolution of mind and heart, of the way man treats man, certainly not to a revolution of violence and destruction. But its spiritual revolution is revolution within a physical world, within a world which—twisted by sin—is still God's world, and the exodus to which it calls is one which must not only lead beyond all known human society but also here and now be lived within human society. I believe that those who refuse to admit any justification for christian revolutionary violence too often either simply fail to see the even spiritually revolutionary character of christianity, identifying it instead with a spirituality of conservatism coupled with compensatory otherworldliness, or suffer from a profound dualism of gospel and world, or nature and grace, which prevents them from providing any convincing ethic of christian participation in this worldly society at any level.[2]

Physical violence is indeed the world at its most worldly, its hardest and cruellest. More than anything else does it jar with the good news of mercy. Of itself it expresses and manifests anything but the christian spirit on its own. Nevertheless the christian spirit does not exist on its own, but within the physical world and it has to be continually incarnated in concrete circumstances which the christian is called to respond to, but in no way controls. The basic type situation here is for a christian to encounter a child being beaten to death: he cannot save the child except by immediate violent intervention. I cannot see that he has other than an absolute duty so to intervene, which means that at times the christian has the duty to take part in physical

[2] Jacques Ellul, *Violence*, London (SCM Press) 1970, is a painful example of the latter kind of thinking. It is full of fallacies in argument and unsound theology, though some of the 'theologians of violence' he criticises may be equally unsound and naive in their interpretation of contemporary events; but Ellul too is naive in his interpretation of history.

violence. Here and now this, and this alone, can properly express christian faith and love.

Colin Morris has recently written: 'If we go by the strict letter of the gospels, neither violent nor non-violent revolutionaries can put Jesus into the witness box on their behalf. He would have no truck with any kind of resistance to evil.'[3] Is this really true? Do the gospels as they stand offer us no ground for resistance to evil? Surely they do. No condemnation of evil could be much stronger than Jesus' condemnation of the Pharisees and of much else. The big question it leaves open is how to incorporate such condemnation into one's own life style, but the fact of utter condemnation is not open to argument. Evidently Jesus does not offer an example of violent resistance to evil; it would not have been appropriate for him to do so. To think that christians as christians can only rightly do some precise thing if they can show that Jesus already did it, is of course an example of a particularly crude type of theology; Morris feels it necessary to try and prove that 'really' Jesus did resist Roman rule. But the implementation of the total gospel in many ages and millions of people cannot possibly look for a precise exemplar in the life of Jesus.

A key principle in gospel morality is the difference between self and neighbour. The Sermon on the Mount certainly puts forward non-resistance as a spiritual ideal where injustice to *self* is concerned, but it has nothing to say about what you do where there is injustice to your neighbour. But the parable of Dives and Lazarus and so much else do. So does James and 1 John. If the supreme law of morality (Mat 25) is to help your neighbour in need, material need, then it naturally follows that you may have at times to take the goods of a third person in order to render that help, or otherwise to act in a violent way. The final law offered by Christ is not one of non-violence nor

[3] C. Morris, *Unyoung, Uncoloured, Unpoor*, London (Epworth Press) 1969.

the respect of property, it is the service of the under-privileged.

There are circumstances in which physical violence may be both permissible and necessary, at the individual level and at the group level. One cannot see why what is moral for the individual should not be so also for the group. In fact, of course, for hundreds of years the vast majority of christians have recognised that this must be so both within the state and, at times, between states. They have accepted this too for many revolutions, at least in retrospect. I find it impossible to believe that they were wholly wrong, even if the application of such principles was indeed more than often disgraceful. But certainly, if one is to condemn violence as necessarily unchristian, one must do it consistently, as Tolstoi did: 'As soon as men understand that their participation in violence is incompatible with the christianity they profess', he wrote, they will 'refuse to serve as soldiers, tax collectors, judges, jury and police agents'.[4] That is logical, though I don't believe it is christianity. But it is not logical to rule out one type of violence as altogether unchristian while supporting all other types.

To consider all violence as out of court for a christian is to take the Sermon on the Mount quite out of context—both out of the complete biblical context and out of the context of world history and world society which we believe to be the only true context in which ultimately to evaluate the teaching of Christ. If it were so, then christianity could either only be the religion of a small, persecuted sect, quite out of the mainstream of the world's life, or it must consistently make for anarchy. I don't believe that this is the religion of the incarnation at all, but Tolstoi's attitude to violence, just as his attitude to sex and much else, was somehow profoundly anti-incarnational.

[4] Leo Tolstoi, *The Law of Love and the Law of Violence*, London (Anthony Blond) 1970.

One must condemn the quite ghastly and ever so frequent aberrations in christian history whereby religion has been used to buttress false nationalisms and causes of every kind. One must beware of thinking of any movement of war or revolution as an ultimate, something above criticism, a god to worship with human sacrifice. One must urge the most stringent and probing examination of any course of violent action before committing oneself to it as a christian; but one cannot rule out the truth that such commitment is nevertheless in many circumstances a necessity for a christian.

As regards the particular case of revolutions, there is no question but that there have been many violent revolutions which have indeed, without inaugurating utopia, yet improved the lot of man very notably, bringing to an end situations of disgraceful injustice. In the words of the famous 1967 *Message to the Third World* of eighteen bishops, 'All revolutions are not necessarily good, but history shows that certain revolutions were necessary and that they freed themselves of their momentary antagonism to religion, yielding good fruits.'

For many young people in Poland, France or Britain in 1939 the moral thing for a christian conscience was to join the armed forces, to commit oneself to an organised endeavour to overthrow with violence a regime of wickedness.[5] Equally in southern Africa in the 1970s the moral thing for many young men may be to join the resistance movements which are endeavouring to overthrow violently the extremely unjust regimes which are dominating South Africa, Rhodesia, Mozambique and Angola. In each case it would be far better if there were a non-violent way to

---

[5] It is worth recalling the words of Karl Barth writing in 1938 from Basle to Professor Hromadka of Prague, 'Every Czech soldier who fights and suffers will be doing so for us too, and—I say this unreservedly—he will also be doing it for the Church of Jesus, which in the atmosphere of Hitler and Mussolini must become the victim of either ridicule or extermination.' (E. Bethge, *Dietrich Bonhoeffer*, London [Collins] 1970, 510.)

achieve the end, but in each case it has become rather clear that there is not and that the organised injustice and institutional violence are so great that an appeal to revolutionary violence is justified and indeed inevitable. In a physical world there come circumstances where the only reasonable thing is to use physical means to overthrow moral evil which has dug itself in physically.

Today as in 1939 many innocent people will as a result be killed and maimed, many beautiful and valuable things will be destroyed; but human society is a vast balance of consent and coercion, justice and freedom, spirit and matter. Where in a particular area it has been set so violently askew by evil-willing men, the balance too can only be restored in a violent way. There does indeed remain a choice in conscience. There were still some in 1939 who found it morally impossible to fight Hitler. They witnessed, often heroically, to the ultimate inadequacy of violence as a means of solving human problems and to the ease with which good men taking up violence can be corrupted and become a mirror of what they are professing to resist. Fighting nazism led to the deliberate monstrosity of the bombing of Dresden, of Würzburg, and so much else: this could be done by a free world acclimatised over several years to the use of violence and corrupted by it. The dossier of the war and post-war crimes of the Allies in the 1940s has yet to be completed. Nevertheless the decision of the majority in 1939 to fight was not an immoral nor an unchristian one, and that decision was not invalidated by crimes subsequently committed by the Allies.

The same sort of decision may have to be come to as regards South Africa today. A fearful tyranny where a small minority of the population has made of the vast majority what is little other than a slave race and where the whole system of government, land apportionment, industry and education is engineered to maintain this, is a monstrosity of the same order as that of the Nazis, though the tactics are admittedly different. The pattern of life and government in Rhodesia is now moving steadily in the direction of that of South Africa. Its bishops have condemned its new laws as 'contrary to the christian faith'. There is one white man in Rhodesia for every twenty black, yet the whites have arrogated to themselves political control of the country and half of all the land. Again, Mozambique and Angola have been for decades lands of blatant oppression, in some ways less unjust than South Africa, but in others still more cruel. In all these countries the basic dignity, human and political, of the great majority of the people is inherently thwarted by the central principles of government. Today the governments and military systems of these four lands are drawing more and more together, and the Cabora Bassa dam project is the symbol of the integration of their politico-economic tyranny. They constitute a single whole, each one rejecting the basic right of the majority of the people within their frontiers to enjoy a full life as political beings. Legitimate opposition has been stifled. There remains for the African no non-violent and constitutional way in which these tyrannies could be overthrown. In these circumstances for the christian, who is a deeply and properly political being, the way of violence can become the moral way and may indeed be the obligatory way.

The governments of these countries are not the state in any moral sense for they do not exist with the genuine support, either explicitly or implicitly given, of the majority of the population and their primary aim is not the good of the whole nation but the maintenance of the privileges of a few. They are a tyranny against which Catholic political theory at any rate has regularly recognised the right of rebellion. In admitting the possible justification of violence one is not, in the order of ideas, being very revolutionary: one is simply applying in the hard world of today sound principles of political order. If a government is deeply unjust and not seeking the common good, St Thomas

Aquinas taught us, there can be a duty of resistance to it.[6] In *Populorum Progressio* Pope Paul has echoed him in agreeing that revolution is justified 'in the case of a manifest and prolonged tyranny that attacks the fundamental rights of the person and endangers the common good of the country'.[7] Pope Paul's presentation of copies of *Populorum Progressio* in July 1970 to Agostinho Neto, president of MLPA, the chief Angolan resistance movement, and Marcellino dos Santos of FRELIMO, cannot be wholly unrelated to a relevant application of this teaching. It is well to remember that Dietrich Bonhoeffer, perhaps the most opportune saint of the twentieth century, was hanged by the state for joining in a plot of violent revolution. He himself had earlier been a pacifist and particular admirer of Gandhi.

To say all this is certainly not to laud the road of revolution over that of reconciliation or that of non-violent resistance. Both the latter must continue to be tried, and especially by those who, outside southern Africa, have greater freedom to manoeuvre. Just because there is so little that the majority can legally do within these countries to change the situation, a very particular obligation is

[6] See A. P. D'Entreves, *The Medieval Contribution to Political Thought*, Oxford 1939, 34–5.

[7] *Populorum Progressio*, 31. For the most part, of course, over the last few hundred years the institutional church has repudiated the Thomist position. It is very interesting to read the remarks of Walter McDonald in *Reminiscences of a Maynooth Professor*, 1925, on the subject of Irish struggles and the failure of the Irish hierarchy to support its own people, above all in the conflicts of the Land League. For instance: 'We were instructed that against legitimate government it is never lawful to rebel. . . . Cardinal Cullen, at that time, gave the tone to the thought of the Irish clergy; and the Cardinal was very much misunderstood if he believed that rebellion may be permissible —if he was not a Tory of the strictest type' (p. 168). 'Boycotting is a revolutionary weapon, and—unfortunately, as I think—the rulers of the Catholic Church have been opposed to revolution in any shape' (p. 331). 'Boycotting, if justifiable at all, is to be justified on the principle of resistance to unjust aggression' (p. 333). 'The older I grow, moreover, the more inclined I become to believe that the people of any country have an equitable right to the land of the country' (p. 335).

placed upon christians and humanists in other countries to exert whatever pressure it is possible to bring. This duty derives from the truly unitary nature of human society. Social and political responsibilities and human brotherhood do not end at state borders. And it is very especially the responsibility of those who do not wish to see violent revolution develop to use every non-violent (or relatively non-violent) means at international level to effect a change of policy. Today the only conceivable alternative to violent revolt locally (built up from immediately neighbouring states) is boycott of trade, sport and art internationally. To condemn both the one and the other and yet still profess to be strongly opposed to the injustice of apartheid is simply not to talk sense at the level of the international moral and political community of which today we are all individually members.

It has to be confessed that these ways have not in fact, been effectively used and when political leaders and practising christians in a country like Britain, which has more opportunity than most to know the true state of affairs in southern Africa, are actually anxious to end even the boycott on arms, then it becomes obvious too that there are others who will arrive at the solid conviction that there is no other way than that of violent revolution. We have sadly but honestly to accept the truth that participation in this world of ours can call the christian even so far, with all the terrible dangers of the weapon corrupting the user, of escalation, of in the end merely replacing one tyranny with another, that this can involve. But in southern Africa the governments of Portugal, South Africa and Rhodesia have deliberately and continually closed the door upon any path to reconciliation in justice. They have escalated the violence of their own regimes. They have made of half a continent a world of injustice, of fear, of a small minority basking in the comfort created by the serfdom of the majority. In such circumstances it is still, let us hope, the mission for some, for many, christians to manifest the way of truth and justice in a wholly non-violent way. But it has become both right and inevitable that other christians should feel, on the contrary, that their call is to join the Freedom Fighters— FRELIMO, MPLA or what have you—and this decision must be recognised as coming within the mainstream of authentic christian response to abominable tyranny.[8]

[8] For a further treatment of this subject I would refer to the sensitive and balanced chapter of Walter Stein entitled 'Mercy and Revolution' in *From Culture to Revolution* ed. T. Eagleton and B. Wicker, London (Sheed & Ward) 1968, 223–246. The following words of President Nyerere, part of his address to Toronto University in October 1969, are also to be commended:

There are some people who appear to believe that there is virtue in violence and that only if a freedom struggle is conducted by war and bloodshed can it lead to real liberation. I am not one of these people; the Government of Tanzania does not accept this doctrine, and nor do any of the other free African Governments as far as I am aware.

We know that war causes immense sufferings, that it is usually the most innocent who are the chief victims, and that the hatred and fear generated by war are dangerous to the very freedom and non-racialism it is our purpose to support. We have a deep desire for a peaceful transfer of power to the people.

But if the door to freedom is locked and bolted, and the present guardians of the door have refused to turn the key or pull the bolts, the choice is very straightforward. Either you accept the lack of freedom or you break the door down.

. . . When every avenue of peaceful change is blocked, then the only way forward to positive change is by channelling and directing the people's fury—that is, by organised violence, by a people's war against their government.

6

THE THEOLOGY OF RACE

I

'Truly I perceive that God shows no partiality' (Ac 10:34). That was the comment of the apostle Peter when, helped by a special insight, he comprehended that the division of Gentile from Jew had ceased to exist. The long years of the Old Testament had been years of apparent partiality, of divine selection: 'I will establish my covenant with you and your descendants' (Gn 17:7). There was Israel, the society of those descendants, originally a racial unity, the chosen people, and there was the rest, the Gentiles, the people without. Certainly the books of the Old Testament have many and increasing universalist breakthroughs. Even Abraham's initial covenant was seen as somehow for the sake of the others: 'In you all the families of the earth shall be blessed' (Gn 12:3). The coming of the Messiah, Isaiah clearly saw, would not affect Israel alone; it would bring 'light to the nations' and in those last days the peoples would come on pilgrimage to Jerusalem—a symbol of visible unity. Certainly there was no trace of apartheid in the final eschatological vision of Israel: 'In those days ten men from the nations of every tongue shall take hold of the robe of a Jew, saying, "Let us go with you, for we have heard that God is with you"' (Zech 8:23). And then they will sit down together at a feast of racial unity: 'On this mountain the Lord of hosts will make for all peoples a feast of fat things, a feast of wine on the lees, of fat things full of marrow, of wine on the lees well refined' (Is 25:6). Eschatological unity, yet actual division. Concretely in the

here and now a sense of exclusiveness and of apartness remained stronger than that of universality, of human togetherness. The covenant of inclusion within the divine
protection did somehow involve for the time being the
exclusion of others. God had shown partiality.

But not now in the time of fulfilment, not 'according to
God's purpose which he set forth in Christ as a plan for
the fullness of time to unite all things in him' (Eph 1:9).
Peter's insight is that Isaiah's age of eschatological racial
unity has somehow arrived. The final plan of God in Christ
can admit no partiality, no exclusion even for the time
being. 'One has died for all' (2 Cor 5:14). For all. And that
new unity of men in the community of salvation has got to
be shown forth at once. For all. Like Peter christians, theologians very much included, have always found it difficult
to take those words quite seriously, quite *au pied de la
lettre*. But the barriers of nation, race, language, country
are all down. To the ends of the earth must the good news
go. Man is one. God is one. Christ is one.

Time after time there has been a tendency to slip back to
a theology of selection and of exclusion. 'We are God's
chosen few, all others must be damned' is a refrain coming
back in one form or another with painful regularity. It is
not, of course, necessarily a racialist attitude, though it is
surprising how often and how quickly it has taken on racial
overtones.[1]

Upon the other side there is the vista of universality, so
vast that it can hardly be comprehended in all its pathways,
but maybe opening suddenly before one at a moment of
unexpected enlightenment: Peter at Caesarea after the roof-
top vision; Paul erupting under a sudden intensity of per-
ception into the heart of human and divine experience:
'God has consigned *all* men to disobedience that he may
have mercy upon *all*. O the depth of the riches and wisdom

[1] The Spanish Inquisition's doctrine of *limpieza* provides an interesting example.

and knowledge of God. How unsearchable are his judg-
ments and how inscrutable his ways' (Rm 11:32-3). John
contemplating the heavenly city: 'Behold, a great multitude
which no man could number, from every nation, from all
tribes and peoples and tongues, standing together before
the throne' (Rev 7:9). Who could really have fathomed
how those long centuries of choice and exclusion and
separation were ephemeral, preparatory only to this fullness of unity, ultimately inadequate as a revelation either
of God or of man? Instead the 'wall of partition' (Eph
2:14) is down, the wall 'between us and them' (Ac 15:9).
Instead we have one and all received the gospel of peace—
'peace for those who are far off', peace for 'those who are
near' (Eph 2:17). Go into all the world and preach the
gospel to the whole of creation: the gospel of peace.

II

The bible begins with Adam and the genealogy of Jesus
too is taken in Luke's gospel back to Adam, son of God
(Lk 3:38). Here again we have the basic concern for all
mankind. It is that which descent from Adam signifies—
unity of all men in nature and need. All exist in the image
of God, all are subject to work and suffering, all die.
Cousins in nature, all are called to be brothers in Christ:
Parthians, Medes, Elamites, ... the Roman centurion, the
Ethiopian minister. One of the most evident implications
of the New Testament is then the total unimportance of
race. Racialism is just self-evidently non-christian, even
though time and again christians have indeed become
racialists—often by thinking themselves back from the New
to a twisted version of the Old Testament situation. Is not
the Faith Europe, and Europe christendom? Have the
natives of America souls? Is not Britain the true Israel?
God's own people and God's own land—God has chosen
us, has given us this land, has made them different, hewers
of wood, drawers of water. Today the psychological division
between 'us' and 'them' may often take in the world at

large a more manifestly racial character than in the past,
but it often tended that way: English and foreigners;
Greeks and barbarians; Aryans and Jews; white and
coloured. The building up of a situation of this kind and
its segregationalist responses is all too characteristic of
human society, but the gospel has its response—a more
explicit response than it has for almost any other social
problem, and that just because the church had to face such
a situation—although one couched in particularly theological terms—right from the word go. Despite hesitations
countenanced by authority and deviationist groups with
their very apartheid line—they refused to eat with the
Gentiles and *separated* themselves (cf. Gal 2:12)—the
church's considered response was uncompromising: 'God
shows no partiality'. The wall is down between 'us and
them'.

Thus the christian church by the most striking facts of
her mission and her earliest crisis in self-awareness has
universalism built into her. The medieval tradition, which
turned the wise men of the Epiphany—the very first gentiles
to worship Christ—into three kings, black, white and
brown, expressed in its simple, popular, grass-roots way the
essential equality of men and of race in the light of Christ,
which is something utterly to be taken for granted within
the church. She has always accepted her mission as one to
all nations and has never admitted racial differences as a
barrier to the christian or human community. But only
since the sixteenth century has she been faced with situations of continuous inter-racial contact on a large scale. It
must be admitted that the result was in many ways not
encouraging. Massacres of Indians, the organised slave
trade, even the denial that these were really men at all.
But the church's voice did not hesitate. Not only cham-
pions like Bartholomew de Las Casas but the pope himself
spoke out with clarity: 'The Indians, though still not
received into the bosom of the church, must not be deprived
of their freedom or possessions, *for they are men*' (Paul III

in 1537). It was the position of the great theologian of natural law, Francisco de Vitoria: natural rights belong to men because they are men, members of a single universal society. They admit of no racial distinction.

Rome's first 'Vicar Apostolic' for Africa was a young Congolese, Prince Henry, consecrated bishop in 1518. Likewise the first vicar apostolic in India was a Brahman convert, Mathew de Castro, appointed in 1637. These were fine gestures, the instinctive movements of the christian mind. They did, alas, remain little more. Further African and Indian bishops were not appointed in the Catholic Church until the twentieth century. The official position of the church was one thing, the pragmatic attitudes and prejudices of most christians another, and in practice the latter widely prevailed. Racial discrimination, even of a blatant kind, has been a notable feature of christian life in many places in modern times—a discrimination which has penetrated even within churches and ecclesiastical institutions of all kinds. Certainly in this matter, as in many others, we have sinned and need to admit it without circumlocution. Today the World Council of Churches, the popes and the Vatican Council have all expressly condemned racial discrimination and that is certainly sincerely endorsed by the vast majority of convinced christians. 'The church rejects, as foreign to the mind of Christ, any discrimination against men or harassment of them because of their race, colour, condition of life or religion.'[2] 'When we are given christian insight the whole pattern of racial discrimination is seen as an unutterable offence against God, to be endured no longer, so that the very stones cry out.'[3] Life and property, all the exigencies of the human condition, fellowship with other men, the highest things and the lowest, the grace of God, the communion of the church—all these things are offered to men without exception because they

[2] *Declaration of the Vatican Council on the Relationship of the Church to Non-Christian Religions*, a.5.
[3] World Council of Churches, Evanston 1954.

are men united in the solidarity of their common divine
image, their common human parentage, their common
redemption.

That is the witness of the christian church and it always
will be so. There can be no walls of separation. The church
does not teach a doctrine of invisible and spiritual things
alone. On the contrary, she witnesses to the incarnation—
to God being with us. We saw him and touched him and ate
and drank with him. Christians are the disciples of Jesus
of Nazareth, those of his company which ate and drank
together in fellowship and must still continue to do so. This
living, human, physical being-together is the sign and
sacrament of all she teaches and means. She cannot teach
a spiritual unity and admit a physical separation. She does
not even start with the spiritual unity; she started with the
physical togetherness of a common board, supper with the
Lord. In the fine words of St Cyprian, repeated and stressed
by the Vatican Council (e.g. in the *Constitution on the
Church*, 9; cf *Constitution on the Liturgy*, 26), the church
is the 'sacrament of unity'. A sacrament is a visible signpost,
a credible manifestation, a showing forth in place and time
such as men can understand. And this unity is a human
one, a unity of men, of the men whom the Lord loves, of all
men. If to deny the spiritual unity and equality of men is
utterly to deny the Bible, to deny that this unity is and
must be manifest in the visible church, to admit apartness
in the visible church though not in the spirit, would be
equally to deny the incarnation, that the Son of God lived
among men, his church a fellowship of men on earth, an
eating and drinking society, a physical-cum-spiritual communion.

The basic physical element linking the initial company
of christians has always to continue. The eucharist supper
is the permanent centre and cause of being of the church:
Do *this* as a memorial of me. Eat. Drink. Together. We are
one body for we share in the one bread. The absolute heart
and essence of christian living is the negation of apartheid:

not uniform belief in the existence of God, but common drinking from a shared cup—the sacrament of unity. It is the unity of men as men in their very animality, and that is made the sign of the union of the spirit. The most earthly communion, the sign of the most divine: the bread we bless and break and eat together is it not a sharing in the body of Christ?

It is a sign with meaning. It really implies unity with God and unity among men. To eat together in church and to remain on principle apart in the seven day a week life whose meaning has to be signed in the Sunday eucharist would be an utter nonsense. It would make of it an empty sign, a farce. Far better not to go to church than to participate in that contradiction in terms, a segregated eucharist, or even in a eucharist for the segregated.

The church then is for all men, for Jew and Greek and Roman and Ethiopian, and its membership essentially involves physical fellowship. The life and unity she offers cannot just be a subject for belief, it must be lived, and lived in the flesh. Otherwise the church is not the church.

Man matters, and the universal brotherhood of man; race does not. That is not only a judgment of philosophical conviction or religious faith. When one has lived for years with people of another race, worked and played and argued and disagreed with them, when one has read together *Antigone* and *Hamlet* and *St Joan*, and shared their struggles and triumphs and emotional crises, and shared one's own with them, then one knows indeed with the conviction of the deepest human experience that men are one, and differences of race slip away into the fringes of insignificance. The death of Socrates is no more mine than theirs. It belongs to all whose humanity is sufficient to share in it and the experience of this joins us together inseparably as men, just as communicating in a common eucharist presenting the death of Jesus Christ joins us utterly as christians.

III

Is there nothing positive to say, then, of race? Is it simply to be dismissed as a false premise for segregation? That can hardly be so. The mystery of human experience is continually one both of unity and of diversity. When we speak of the first Adam, the historically first being who had a human destiny, and our common unity in him, we speak of a unity of poverty, of possibility, of what can become. When we speak of the second Adam and the uniting of all things in him who is Omega, we speak instead of a unity of fullness, of realisation, of varied development. The unity of the last times is one of harvest, good measure pressed down and flowing over. Between one and the other there must have been a vast multiplication of diversity—the growing up of humanity, a growing up which involves too a growing apart. The diversity of mankind, the non-uniformity, is as significant as its unity; regimentation as criminal as enforced separation. Man must be man, not just *in globo*, but in the development of his individual nature and personality. Each is other, and this otherness penetrates all through us, all through the complex of the spiritual and the material that is a human being. We cannot be other in the spirit, but utterly uniform in the flesh. For we are enfleshed spirit, rational animals. Just as the unity of fellowship cannot be one of the spirit alone but must be incarnated in physical life, so must our diversity—variety in mind, but variety too in our very animality.

The range of physical variety in mankind is the essential manifestation of this aspect of the human condition. The different features of the members of a single family, the similarities, the strange combinations, the seemingly endless variety even within the range of a particular type of human physique; the slightly wider differences, at the national or regional level, the blond Scandinavian, the black Spaniard; then the full racial contrasts, deeper physical variations between the historically more distant branches of the human family; and always within each group an equal range of personal diversification: all this is the physical expression of the innate vocation of man to be himself, to be sacramentally different and recognisable from his fellows.

Race shows man as truly animal. We have no reason to be ashamed of this. Just as there are different breeds of dogs, so are there different breeds of men. We demonstrate our collegiality with the animal world by being ourselves racially diverse. All animal groups have this diversity within the species, and if man is truly a 'rational animal' then mankind must share in a pattern of physical diversity relating to lineage groups. 'Man' in fact cannot be understood without 'race'—at least unless we believe in a neoplatonic soul-man. If man is body too, if he is animal, then he is racial. This is by no means his most significant characteristic but it is truly and necessarily part of him. The having of race is not an extra over and above a full anthropology, it is implied in a sound anthropology.

Indeed the various racial characteristics, certainly related in one way or another with the climate and physical pressures of different parts of the world, precisely express our individual human entity as being truly a participation in the physical cosmos, an 'existence-in-the-world': part of the world, not just somewhat awkwardly placed here in a vale of tears to pass the span of our mortal existence, but truly growing and belonging here, being moulded and varied according to the pressures of wind and rain and sun, just like brother dog and brother horse.

But the enormously much greater complexity of variety in human features represents the enormously much greater richness of the human vocation. Like the animals, we express ourselves in physical features moulded by the forces of biology and geography working over the generations, but moulded too by personal character and experience, by work, by knowledge, by love. The physical diversity of men, from the bones to the twist of the lip, is the sacrament of human existence: the visible expression of intelligent beings fully participating in a material and animal world.

IV

The fact of race is then to be recognised as, in a way, the typical manifestation of our created existence being a fully-of-this-world existence, and to be ashamed of it or to want to ignore it is really the expression of a manichaean or pseudo-platonist view of a man as spirit alone, somehow contaminated by being subject to the conditions of physical animality.

We accept it: race is part of being man. Having recognised this we can see the danger arising of a false conclusion, the type of conclusion often drawn and somehow justifying racial segregation. Race is part of man, we say. It is then part of the natural order, God's plan for the world. Now modern conditions are mixing the races; they are producing inter-racial marriages, inter-racial societies. This development is confusing God's plan. On the contrary the natural order must be maintained: the races must be held apart. Apartheid is then a policy of human cooperation with the natural law of God.

A conclusion of this kind results from grave over-simplifications concerning the social consequences of a physical condition, the moral objectivisation of a particular historical state of man, and indeed the whole conception of 'being natural'.

When we say that having race is part of the nature of man, we are talking about a physical condition not a social or cultural one. Historically the division of races has in fact corresponded to some extent with geographical and cultural divisions. That correspondence was natural too—using 'natural' in a rather different sense: that is to say it was suitably characteristic of a certain not very evolved state of human society. Thus it is natural to use one's legs to move from one place to another, yet using a car is also natural;

it follows from the whole nature of man—not only a two-legged animal but also an intelligent being, one able to adapt other material things and circumstances to satisfying his needs.

Again, it is 'natural' to be of a race, but it is equally 'natural' to be able to marry someone of another race. Such observations indicate one aspect or another of our being, they don't evidently imply one or another over-all line of conduct. A half-caste is as 'natural' as someone of pure race. A study of these things throws light on what we are, but it cannot create an imperative to maintain a particular condition.

The trouble here, as in so many fields, is to identify the 'natural' (with a consequential moral law) with the historically prior condition, or with what is guessed to have been the historically prior condition. There is always a strong temptation to do this—to think of the natural as the original and primitive pattern rather than as the condition which best expresses the inherent potentialities of such and such a being. One is Hobbes' state of nature, the other Aristotle's. For the latter nature is to be found in the end.[4] Man is a social being and both in himself and in society he can only express himself, he can only fully be himself across a process of evolution, of the growth of human consciousness and human skills within a developing society. Man, segregated in his racial group and knowing only his own language, controlled in his life by the physical elements, using a few implements upon which he has imprinted his own character only very faintly, is man

---

[4] Gandhi's morality was a good example of the fallacious identification of the natural with the primitive. Hence his condemnation of railways: 'God set a limit to a man's locomotive ambitions in the construction of his body . . . railways are a most dangerous institution. Man has gone further away from his Maker'. So many discussions in ethics and moral theology derive from contradictory views (static versus evolutionary) of human nature. Hobbes, of course, while identifying the natural with the primitive, did not in the least identify the moral with the natural.

unevolved, largely unaware of himself, near the start of his providential pilgrimage. On the other hand, man who is the master of a mass of techniques which he has drawn out of the inter-action of his own intelligence and the world about him, who can share fellowship with men of origin far from his own, this 'modern man' (full of dangers certainly—of possibilities for evil and cruelty and the final disaster of de-humanised enslavement to the very things he has created as means for humanisation) is nevertheless—so long as he can remain equal to his condition—vastly more natural than the other. He is living in a condition which he himself has made through activity natural to him, not in a condition in which he is simply found.

A healthy human society cannot but evolve, and in evolving it cannot but push outwards, link itself with other societies, grow with them into one, share and communicate and overflow: and this at every level of religion and philosophy and law and language and commerce and race. Man must mix and share, Mercians with Wessex men, French with English, European with African. The exigencies of human life and society necessitate it. Contact, of course, occasions conflicts, the building up of group rivalries, the fear of ones own identity being endangered. But the process is a continuous and inevitable one within human history and it is a condition for the full 'naturalisation' of man, the achievement of a full humanity.

The moral category 'natural to man' has as its absolute the still unknown end, but concretely its significance is then within a process of becoming, it cannot be validly assessed as an unchanging norm. Its understanding and application involve a historical context. In the year 10,000 BC a thousand things, which we see as fully natural, even 'natural rights', would have seemed infallibly un-natural and quite preposterous and would indeed have been quite un-natural to man then—totally unrelated to his being and to his assessment of himself within the historical and social context that man was then in.

The process historical man is within, or perhaps better the process which he is—despite regressions and sidesteps and pauses—producing out of himself, out of his needs and urges and aptitudes, is one growing together, not in absolute uniformity, but in a complex inter-dependent diversity. Historically the type of diversity based upon 'separate development' and a rather low degree of external influence, which was characteristic of an early stage of human society, is everywhere giving way to a diversity of continuous interpenetration. This is shown as inevitable by a study of the history of human society as we know it, but it can equally be seen to be demanded by a study of man as a social being, requiring as he grows in competence a society of ever-increasing dimensions. Developed man cannot not live within a world society.

This is called for too by the nature of Christianity, of the realised participation of all humanity in the New Adam and within the church. From the very earliest times she has been entitled 'catholic'; *Catholic Church* means 'World Assembly' and men cannot be assembled within the ecclesial fellowship if they are humanly and socially sundered. The church is the salt and the ideal and the 'so-much-more-beyond' of human society, not its antithesis.

Now the human quality of race must be seen within this whole vista of man-in-evolution, on pilgrimage. As a part of our nature, it is not to be torn apart and treated differently from the rest of how we are. Moreover, since flesh must serve spirit, and this is as such so utterly characteristic of the flesh, of being animals, it has above all to serve the spiritual kingdom, the full advance of mankind in unity and truth, not be set apart as an object of adoration or of fear or of division.

Racially separate communities were characteristic of a rather unevolved pattern of human society. They are incompatible with a highly articulated and extended one. Today human society requires interpersonal and intergroup contact on a vast scale—at the level of mind and

research, of commerce, of eating together, of love. We meet
as men fully, not as minds only or as a market for consumer
goods. In the process of historical evolution which we share
in, we have reached today the building of a single world
society not in theory but in fact. We see this as demanded
both by the facts of the contemporary situation—demo-
graphic, educational, economic, political—and by a full
conception of what man is. But building a single world
society of man necessarily means building an inter-racial
society, just because man is a multi-racial being. To be fully
man today, in the last third of the twentieth century, sharing in the 'natural' condition for contemporary man, means
to share and willingly in inter-racial society. This has now
become quite simply our *Sitz im Leben*.

As a member of the church one's vocation in this age is
directly related to this. For the church—which is people,
God's people, God's people here and now—is necessarily
an 'in-this-world' reality, her historical being controlled by
the historical condition of human society. The world does,
after all, write the church's agenda in every age, and in this
age the agenda it has written for us is clearly an inter-racial
one. In doing so it does not more than explicitate her own
inherent nature. The church witnesses to the world, but in
doing so grows in the realisation of her own very being.
Always in principle the Catholic fellowship, by her calling
a world society of redeemed men, she was not able to be
this in act, in an achieved way, when there could not exist
a world society. The present historical condition of
humanity is really making it possible for the first time for
the universal church to be herself: not merely to have
members of many lands and races, but truly to be a fellowship, a lived communion, of all nations—the sacrament of
unity: that is to say a full visible, manifest and credible
sign of a human fellowship of love without bars and dis-
criminations joining all God's children. As racial characteristics are the most visible sign of difference and division
within mankind and today present psychologically the

greatest cause of separation and conflict, so it is intrinsically required that if the church is to be a worldwide signpost of divine and human unity and that effectively for today, then she must above all be seen as an inter-racial fellowship. This is not marginal to today's church: it forms on the contrary the very core of the contemporary agenda, the point on which we today will stand or fall. Such is what it means to be the 'sacrament of unity' in the twentieth century.

Moreover, as the local church is the microcosm of the universal church, truly manifesting the character of the latter, so it is positively required that in an inter-racial area the local church too appears as an inter-racial communion, sacrament of unity for these men here. Failure to do this is failure to be the church.

One God, one Lord, one Spirit, one destiny, yes but one flesh too: one incarnate Lord, and so one physical fellowship, one eating and drinking together. We who are many and diverse in skin and hair and jaw are one body, for we all partake of one bread.

7

TOWARDS A SPIRITUALITY OF THE ROAD

'Home is behind, the world ahead.' These words from one of Bilbo Baggins's journey songs in Prof. Tolkien's masterpiece, *The Lord of the Rings*,[1] have brought into my mind a trail of thoughts concerning those two poles of earthly life—home and the world. There is such a continual play of forces deriving from one or the other, and such a straining of man between these rival loyalties, that it deserves our consideration. The great epics are constructed around this central tension, and their old themes remain ever fresh in human imagination and experience. Bilbo's own adventure, in the earliest of Tolkien's histories of the Third Age, entitled *The Hobbit*, was a happy 'There and Back Again,' and his journey song could end with the turned refrain 'world behind and home ahead', but all do not return like Bilbo or Ulysses to the hearth and all those good things fought for and left behind, doubly dear now after sight of the Beyond. *The Lord of the Rings* tells of adventures far more serious than those of *The Hobbit*, little wonder if they left a deeper mark; Frodo, Bilbo's heir, the Free World's Ring-Bearer, triumphed indeed on Mount Doom against all expectation, and even returned for a short while to the well-loved Shire. But if his home of Bag End had changed relatively little, Frodo himself had changed too much; he was one of those heroes not destined to enjoy again the old, quiet things, the local heaven he had entered the wild to

---

[1] Part One, *The Fellowship of the Ring*, p. 87.

save. Deeply wounded by the world's contact, sacrificed for the Shire, he must sail away with the Elves to the Western lands.

Journeying has meaning deeper than we may imagine. Its sense is found in contrast to that of the home. All through the ages (wrote Fr Gerald Vann),[2]

> the home has been both a reality of profound importance in its own right, and at the same time a symbol of profound significance. The walls are the symbol of the family's security from enemies and wild beasts without, and of its own unity within; the window is the symbol of vision, for the family must not be turned in upon itself but must look out upon the greater world, on the garden, the field, and thence to the wider, distant horizons, and in the end to the eternal hills, and the door is the symbol of that adventuring forth into life without which life can never be lived in its fullness, an adventuring which must somehow involve the sacrifice of security. . . .

We need to recapture a theological sense of the home, but—still more—of its necessary opposite: the venturing forth from the family circle into the world beyond. They are key symbols in human experience.

There is always the kind of man intended to enjoy the home values, the milieu of a Trollope or a Jane Austen, the settled order of the *polis*, the little enlightened world centre walled off from outer turmoil,[3] and there is the kind of man who, often in spite of himself, must go afar off in search of

> . . . the hidden paths that run
> Towards the Moon or to the Sun,

the paths of adventure, or souls, or money, or just distant things and a life unusual. 'One of these two fates is the best

[2] *The Water and the Fire*, p. 15.
[3] The best pictorial representation of this which I remember is the village in the Japanese film, *The Seven Samurai*.

fate for every man. Either to be what I have been, a
wanderer with all the bitterness of it, or to stay at home
and hear in one's own garden the voice of God.' The words
are Belloc's,[4] a wanderer in spite of all his love for Sussex
Downs.

Certainly the christian transformation of human things
never levels an old structure, but renews it from cellar to
attic, with higher meaning and more enduring value. So
this dichotomy will remain, and there will still be two
ways and the wrench of the old loves to be experienced and
mastered within a pattern of ecclesial living. It is true that
there has been a tendency to shape the whole upon the
home design, while what canon law knows as the *peregrinus,*
and still more the *vagus,* has been an object of suspicion.
Spirituality in this field has not been far different from the
law; it is characterised by the monastery and the novitiate,
of all places the most fixed. Both stem from the fixity of a
church conceived as a 'perfect society'. One may find a loss
here. Our Lord had 'nowhere to lay his head,' and to sanc-
tify sinners he 'suffered beyond the city gate'. The call to
that beyond, outside the walls of the old-loved city, is an
essential part of the christian life; it explains and it exacts
the pilgrim and the missionary, who have gone out from
home and left the home values behind them. What a pity
that the missionary way can be wholly ignored in such a
christian classic as the *Imitation of Christ,* and that what
has passed as missionary spirituality has very often been no
more than a misplaced copy of the home variety.

We stand in need of a theology—and also a spirituality—
of journeying, an intrinsically suitable occupation in a
pilgrim church. It is true that Baedeker, modern technology
and travel agencies seem to have made a long and uncertain
journey of the old sort quite a rare experience. It is true
that space travel is beginning to provide a new opening
here. But the total time spent on travelling now is not less

4 From *The Death of Wandering Peter* in *On Something.*

than before; rather the contrary, and there are a vast number of people, including many priests and lay apostles, who live the greater part of their time away from home, always hurrying to conferences, tours of inspection, or special missions; they are up-rooted, and necessarily suffer in their souls the effect of this external instability.

It is in the monastic and Benedictine tradition that I find the purest form of the home type of christian living. The vow of *Stabilitas* is characteristic of a whole approach to the art of life. It has been well said that the spirit of the Benedictine community approximates more than that of any other order to the spirit of the natural family. Here all the natural values of the local community are carried up into a higher, explicitly God-centred way of life. Belonging to a fixed place is of the essence, and in a way we may say that it is the hermit who is most at the centre of this approach to things. His place is smaller, he is more strictly localised. Unfortunately the hermit idea too has been under a cloud in the christian west; it has been largely replaced by a purely cenobitical ideal; but it would, I think, be a mistake to believe that the latter is entirely faithful to St Benedict's own view; the Father of western monks neither disowned his personal experience at Subiaco nor denied the traditional doctrine of the superiority of the eremitical vocation;[5] perhaps more room will need to be found for this in the future. Among hermits the most localised was of course the Stylite. With him, one feels, the home sense has been wholly stylised and supernaturalised, but in the varied field of christian experience he is there to give naked witness to the human and spiritual value of a fixed abode. A more easily appreciable instance of the sanctity of the local and the uneventful might be found in St Alphonsus Rodriguez . . .

[5] See an article entitled *St Benedict and the Eremitical Life*, Downside Review, 1950, pp. 191–211.

4

Yet God . . .
Could crowd career with conquest while there went
Those years and years by of world without event
That in Majorca Alfonso watched the door.

If the supernatural at times works according to natural tendencies, at others it demands a complete reversal. The man with the stay-at-home temperament (like Habacuc) is carried off with a missionary vocation to the ends of the earth, while the natural vagabond requires the chastening of a settled monastic discipline. Moreover in an individual context the monastic vocation requires an initial home-separation, and may later through obedience require others. But it does create a new earthly home, and the monastery is the typical milieu for home spirituality, just as the mission is for road spirituality. The trouble is that the monastery, instead of offering one pattern of spiritual living, has, at least until recently, been allowed to dominate the whole. It is curious how monastic the way of life of friars and Jesuits has become, besides that of many more recent missionary societies. The whole tendency can be seen as a failure at the level of spirituality to accept the pilgrim nature of the church.

The missionary vocation involves rejection of the home values. Its point of departure may be found in verse 10 of Psalm 44. 'Listen, daughter, see and attend: forget your people and your father's home.' Hard command and one not always faithfully followed. All the sad history of that missionary nationalism which has at times so grievously affected apostolic work comes from failure to understand this first of laws: 'Forget your people and your father's home.' The missionary must be someone who goes out not only physically but also culturally and psychologically from the homeland; a new Abraham. 'Leave thy country and thy land and thy neighbour in the flesh and thine own father-land for my sake and get thee into the country that I will show thee.' In his *Life of St Columcille* a Middle-Irish writer commented on this verse thus: 'Now the good action which God enjoined upon the father of the faithful, that is, on Abraham, is a duty for his sons after him, that is on all the faithful, to fulfil: to leave their soil and their land, their wealth and their worldly joy for the sake of the Lord of the elements and to go into perfect exile in imitation of him.'[6] 'The folk of perfect pilgrimage' were particularly numerous in the Ireland of the first christian centuries. Wandering is an Irish trait both natural and supernatural, but it is linked with the dearest love for the land left behind. We can learn much of the spirit of the missionary from the christian Irish of the early days, of those who set off on the *Peregrinatio pro Christo*. For them, and equally for the early English christians, the missionary pilgrimage entered right into the marrow of life in Christ; there was a duty both to carry the faith to others, and to separate oneself from the dearest of things, the homeland. They were caught up in the *consuetudo peregrinandi*, and the greatest of them—a Columbanus or a Boniface—evangelised the whole of Europe, but while making of Europe a home for the faith they found never a home for themselves; they embraced the enduring martyrdom of exile.

The life of such men was inevitably different from that of the well-ordered monastery or pious establishment, although they left a whole chain of such institutions behind them. This life of road and ship has a long line of characteristic heroes: Frances Xavier, tossing in the heat of the Eastern seas, alone with a pagan crew on the route to Japan; Benedict Joseph Labre, the pure wanderer whose peregrinations were unlinked with apostolate; Francis of Assisi, who belongs so completely to the pilgrim side of christian life that it is strange to find that the Franciscan convent has become the most rooted of elements in an Italian countryside. St Francis and his early followers were among those who have chosen the world rather than the

[6] Quoted by Robin Flower, *The Irish Tradition*, p. 20.

home. Two lovely incidents may be taken to illustrate this side of early Franciscanism. One is the story in Giovanni Parenti's *Sacrum Commercium* of how Lady Poverty was entertained by the brethren. After a meal and a sleep on the bare ground, she 'rose up after a short space and asked them to show her their monastery. And they brought her to a certain hill and, showing her all the world that might be seen from there, they said: "This is our monastery, Lady!"' The other story is that of the conversation, recorded in the *Fioretti*, between St Francis and Brother Leo on the road from Perugia to St Mary of the Angels. It is found in Chapter VIII and entitled 'How, as St. Francis and Brother Leo were going by the way, he set forth unto him what things were perfect joy.'

Brother Leo with much marvel besought him, saying: 'Father, I pray thee in the name of God that thou tell me, wherein is perfect joy.' And St. Francis thus made answer: 'When we come to St. Mary of the Angels, all soaked as we are with rain and numbed with cold and besmirched with mud and tormented with hunger, and knock at the door of the house; and the porter comes in anger and says: "Who are ye?" and we say: "We be two of your brethren": and he says, "Ye be no true men; nay, be two rogues that gad about deceiving the world and robbing the alms of the poor; get ye gone": and thereat he shuts to the door and makes us stand without in the snow and the rain, cold and a-hungered, till night-fall; if there-withal we patiently endure such wrong and such cruelty and such rebuffs without being disquieted and without murmuring against him; and with humbleness and charity bethink us that this porter knows us full well and that God makes him to speak against us; O brother Leo, write that herein is perfect joy. And if we be instant in knocking and he come out full of wrath and drive us away as importunate knaves, with insults and buffetings, saying: "Get ye gone hence, vilest of thieves, begone to the

alms-house, for here ye shall find nor food nor lodging";
if we suffer this with patience and with gladness and with
love, O brother Leo, write that herein is perfect joy.'

This is a peak of missionary spirituality; but if we do not
contemplate the peaks, will we ever ascend even the lower
slopes? The road pointed out by St Francis was nothing
new, and for the classical description of missionary life we
must return to St Paul.

I have toiled harder, spent longer days in prison, been
beaten so cruelly, so often looked death in the face. Five
times the Jews scourged me, and spared me but one lash
in the forty; three times I was beaten with rods, once I
was stoned; I have been shipwrecked three times, I have
spent a night and a day as a castaway at sea. What journeys I have undertaken, in danger from rivers, in danger
from robbers, in danger from my own people, in danger
from the Gentiles; danger in cities, danger in the wilder-
ness, danger in the sea, danger among false brethren! I
have met with toil and weariness, so often been sleepless,
hungry and thirsty; so often denied myself food, gone
cold and naked. And all this, over and above something
else which I do not count; I mean the burden I carry
every day, my anxious care for all the churches.

[2 Cor 11 : 23–8]

St Paul was in all this no more than faithful to the steps of
the Master: 'Foxes have holes, and the birds of the air their
resting-places; the Son of man has nowhere to lay his head'
(Luke 9 : 58).

In the life of the road and the ship prayer is quite as
necessary as in a monastery, but it is easy to see that it will
need to follow a pattern of its own. Tiredness and a multi-
plicity of preoccupations can make formal meditation quite
ineffective. Often no more than the repetition of ejacula-
tions may be possible, but this can well lead straight to the
prayer of quiet. Such prayer, linked with weariness, great
gaiety and the zeal of an 'anxious care for all the churches'

are chief among the characteristics of missionary spirituality.

Is all this fantastically unreal, ideas of a dream-world far removed from the modern efficiency of RAPTIM and the APF?[7] Some may think so, but they should remember that I wish to suggest the pattern of a type of life, and this at its noblest and most meaningful, not to describe the details of a missionary's day in 1970. Yet there are not a few missionaries who could truthfully apply 2 Corinthians 11 to their own experiences in the last years with but little alteration. But it is certainly true that for the most part the missionary in every age must not be a continual wanderer, rather someone who having gone into exile from his own land enters a strange society and genuinely makes it his own in order to serve it. Matthew Ricci went far indeed, but on arrival in Peking his wanderings ended and he set about becoming Chinese. In this way the missionary would seem to re-enter the home-centred life. And, of course, in part he does. Home and the world are inextricably bound together in everyman's life. Yet 'how is it possible that a man should be born when he is already old?' Human nature is an unmalleable thing and *caelum non animum mutant qui trans mare currunt*, or, as Ptolemy remarked, 'A man who has gone into a different climate changes his nature in part. But he cannot change altogether, for in his life's beginning the destiny of his body was determined.'[8] With a vast and most necessary effort the missionary can partially comprehend and adapt himself and enter in, but even if he have the genius of a Ricci, he cannot cease deep down to be what he was, and therefore he remains pilgrim and exile. However long his stay in any one place be in fact prolonged, the aim of a missionary's work must always be to make himself redundant, free to set out elsewhere, to take again to the road.

Road and the home, *Via* and *Patria*, these indicate then

---

[7] RAPTIM: a travel agency which arranges cheap journeys for missionaries. APF: Association for the Propagation of the Faith, a mission aid society.

[8] Quoted by Flower, *op. cit.*, p. 39.

two poles of human and christian experience. The present world is our home and yet it is not. At the deepest level all christian life on earth must be seen as *via*, the road onwards to the heaven which alone is *patria*; and when one is journeying there are two great mistakes that one can make; one is to settle down in a way-side inn before arriving at the true destination, to be satisfied with a half-way house. This is the great temptation of the monastic and settled form of religious life. The other mistake is to forget that journeys are only made for destinations, that activity can have no value apart from contemplation and possession, and that we can cross all the seas and remain without charity. This is the temptation of the missionary life, and is illustrated in another form by the Modernist bishop to be met in C. S. Lewis's fantasy *The Great Divorce*, whose motto was that 'to travel hopefully is better than to arrive'; we wander because the world is unsatisfactory, the danger is to grow satisfied with our wanderings.

We have seen that the missionary life does not exclude something of a home-finding, nor does the monastic life exclude the martyrdom of exile or the necessity of travel. So many of the great missionaries of the past were in fact Benedictines, abandoning their cloistered stability for the salvation of souls. The two lives may be combined, and often the greatest wanderers, men like that dear Englishman of the twelfth century, St Godric of Finchale, make the best hermits.

But in the last resort integration must come at a deeper level, in that very ordering of life between earth and heaven of which I have already spoken. But here still two approaches are possible, corresponding to the two mistakes. One prepares for a new earth by forming on this earth an image of what is to come, the Jerusalem which is on high. Earthly life is a beginning of paradise, a *quaedam inchoatio* of what in its fullness can only be entered into beyond the river of death; the earthly family, whether natural, parochial, monastic or political, prepares one for the family life of the Blessed Trinity. The missionary approach is in itself different, obviating the dangers of attachment to this worldly society which from being an image can become so easily a substitute. On the one side, by moving from one local church to another, the missionary's witness is meant to counterbalance the nationalism which so easily and regularly eats its way into the spiritual life of the fixed religious. His function in the church is to confound every attempt to identify the christian *patria* with the English, the Irish, the German or the French tradition. Beyond this, he has somehow to embody the ultimately pilgrim character of christian existence. The pilgrim sees the earth sternly as *via*, something to be passed through, never a place to pitch tents or settle down while the Jordan of death is still to cross. Frightened of losing courage for the journey through too long a halt in the warm hearth light of any temporal home, the missionary must hurry on along the old road with his eyes on the distant light ahead: *Per tuas semitas duc nos quo tendimus ad lucem quam inhabitas.* The dark roads, the roads which only God knows, the unexpected turnings of the unfamiliar scene, the constant weariness: this is the lot, not only of the missionary, but of every man in the earthly exodus.

> The Road goes ever on and on
> Down from the door where it began.
> Now far ahead the Road has gone,
> And I must follow, if I can,
> Pursuing it with eager feet, . . .

Just another of Bilbo's songs to encourage us on our way.[9]

It is true that every individual christian life draws its justification and its meaning from its power to express some facet of the whole reality of life in Christ, because no single creature can image all. It is the special missionary function to symbolise and show forth the viatory character of everyone's religion, as it is for another man to manifest the con-

[9] *The Fellowship of the Ring*, p. 44.

secration of work, and another to bear the better part of Mary. 'Lead kindly light,' the pilgrim prays, 'amid the encircling gloom, lead thou me on; the night is dark, and I am far from home, lead thou me on.' But Jordan will be crossed, and when the gospel has been preached to every creature and the Son of man returns, pray God that, all journeys over and the home-haven reached, 'we may merrily meet in Heaven'.

8

THE THEOLOGICAL PROBLEM OF
MINISTRIES IN THE CHURCH

It is axiomatic that there is a great difference between what
can be said absolutely about the church's ministry regard-
less of century and country: that it be in obedience to God,
as known to us through the clear teaching of scripture, the
constant witness of tradition and the most authoritative
declarations of the living church from time to time—and
the sociological pattern of ministry in any given time and
place. There can be no possible doubt that the latter can
and should change vastly according to the diverse historical character of the world to which the church must
minister; equally there is no doubt that it has so changed
again and again. It would, then, be quite implausible to
hold that the particular pattern which evolved in western
Europe in, say, the period 1815–1939 on late medieval and
Tridentine foundations has any particular claim to be
normative. Faced with the obvious truth (frequently referred
to in Vatican ii documents, notably *Gaudium et Spes*) that
human society is at present undergoing an unprecedentedly
rapid period of change, it is clear *a priori* that this must
entail very considerable changes in the sociological pattern
of the church's ministry.

The task of the present chapter is neither a theological
study of the ministry and its many problems for its own
sake, nor is it an examination of which structural changes
could be necessary or valuable today for the renewal of the
ministry; instead its aim is simply to outline such theological conclusions as would seem particularly relevant as

ground for that renewal. It is clear that only such doctrinal positions can be 'passed on' as a basis for pastoral renewal as are theologically more or less unquestionable. To take an example: it is held by some who have studied the ministry of the very early church (Küng, in particular) that there were no 'ordained' ministries in the early Pauline churches; that non-ordained christians presided at the eucharist in the first years of the church of Corinth, and that 'presbyters' were only introduced there later, after Paul's death. If such a position were to be accepted as certain, it might have very considerable practical implications. However, as it is, in fact, historically and doctrinally questionable, it is not possible to make present use of it in re-shaping our pattern of ministry.

This study will proceed by considering various issues which combine theological content and current practical significance. Basic to the whole discussion is the recognition that the entire church, the whole people of God, truly participates in the priesthood and mission given to all by Christ and communicated to each in baptism and confirmation; that the activation of this common participation is achieved in many ways, some of which are particular to certain individuals and which we call ministries; and that the shaping of the latter is achieved by God both through the known structures of the church, hierarchically commissioned, and through the unpredictable inspiration of God in particular people and circumstances.

A first theme concerns the internal ordering of the threefold commissioned ministry of bishops, presbyters, deacons. This pattern clearly emerged during the early dynamic years of the church's growth. It was fixed before a hundred years had passed and it has basically remained ever since. It is reaffirmed by chapter 3 of the Dogmatic Constitution *Lumen Gentium*. It would not be theologically acceptable to initiate pastoral reforms which did not respect it, though it must be candidly admitted that in a great part of the church the third—diaconate—level was in fact atrophied for centuries (unless, indeed, the diaconate is ultimately to be interpreted as meaning every serious ministry of service in the church, or at least every such ministry as has been given some type of ecclesial commissioning; and such an interpretation is not impossible).

The acceptance of the commissioned ministry and its threefold shape has, however, few precise implications as to how the ministry is in practice structured. It is clear that a collegial relationship both between and within the ministry of local churches is required, but this too can take many different forms. Theology has nothing decisive to say on such questions as whether a normal diocese will be a community with a ministry of ten presbyters or a thousand; it cannot settle whether a bishop should be the settled head of a small local church or an itinerant overseer of many local churches; it has nothing certain to offer as to whether a bishop is to be chosen by the laity of the local church, or by its clergy, by neighbouring bishops, or again at the level of the universal church. He has in some way to represent the local church within the world communion, just as he represents the total apostolic mandate at local level, but various ways of selection and styles of life are honourably consistent with such requirements.

Again, though theology does suggest that the term 'local church' refers at times more properly to something bigger than a single diocese (to a province or patriarchate in fact) it cannot formulate the juridical character of such a unit or lay down what authority a local synod may have over the individual bishop, though it does say with certainty that there is and must be authority over the individual bishop, and there has always been so.

In the relationship of episcopate and presbyterate an important particular instance is provided by confirmation. The theology of this sacrament remains somewhat confused; not the least part of this confusion is the nature of its relationship with the episcopal office. This relationship hardened in the western church until it could be expressed almost dogmatically at Trent (Denzinger 873). This ignored the eastern experience which had moved in a contrary direction. It is well known that the early drafts of Vatican II's *De Ecclesia* reiterated the Tridentine formula that bishops were the 'ordinary' ministers of confirmation. Confronted with the eastern tradition, this was reformulated as 'original ministers' (*Lumen Gentium*, a. 26). In the same way the early drafts of the Decree on Eastern Churches equally affirmed that the bishop was the 'sole ordinary minister of the sacrament of chrism'. This was simply removed from the final document. The pastoral practice of the western church had already been noticeably modified in this matter by a decree of Pius XII in 1946. Today, theologically speaking, it is an entirely open matter whether in a local church the normal minister of confirmation be a presbyter or a bishop. Pastoral considerations must prevail. In a diocese with a few thousand christians only, the normal retention of the bishop as minister may be a valuable way of maintaining a personal relationship between christians and their chief local pastor. In a diocese of millions, the same retention may be a meaningless formality.

Here, as almost everywhere, the bishop-presbyter balance is in principle an extremely flexible one. Only as regards ordination must current Catholic theology insist that, while the question is wide open for theological discussion, it is not at present open pastorally: ordinations to the presbyterate must be performed by a bishop. Elsewhere, in almost every case it can be that the final answer as regards the relating of bishops and presbyters in liturgy and sacrament, pastoral work, election and decision making, must depend upon the human and pastoral needs of the living church, local and universal.

A second theme is that of the relationship between ordained and non-ordained ministries. It is clear that the earliest books of the New Testament present us with a rich diversity of ministries and that some of these, at least, were clearly not associated with the laying on of hands. The contrast between the image of how a local church may be ordered as found in 1 Corinthians is strikingly different from that presented a good many years later by the Pastorals. What is most certainly significant in the evidence of 1 Corinthians is its positive, not its negative, aspect. In fact Acts also presents considerable evidence of a wide diversity of ministries. The Pastorals and the letters of Ignatius suggest an impoverishment here: the 'hierarchical' structure has somehow eaten up the other ministries (that, at least, is the impression they give). This could already easily point towards a church wherein only a minority of members are really expected to exercise an active mission, just as (somewhat later) only a minority came to be expected to seek something described as 'perfection' or, again, exercise their universal priesthood.

Vatican II has explicitly recognised that within the church there is a variety of ministries (*Lumen Gentium*, a. 18; *Apostolicam Actuositatem*, a. 2) corresponding to a variety of charisms. This is scripturally and theologically certain, and it is clear that the greater part of the activities normally associated with a priest's life in modern times can as fittingly be related to the non-ordained ministries: pastoral work of many kinds, teaching the faith to catechumens and to the young, visiting the sick, marriage counselling, administering church goods. In fact for many years such ministries have been regularly performed by catechists and nuns. What the basic theological relationship of these ministries is to the historic 'diaconate' is not yet clear. *Lumen Gentium* a. 29 presents immediate pastoral guidance in a time of transition rather than a final doctrinal statement.

Historically it is clear that the tendency of the presbyteral ministry to 'eat up' other ministries and consequently create a rather clear division within the church between ministers and those ministered to has been a repeated one. In subsequent centuries the tendency towards the monoformity of the apostolic age has been repeated. In the third and fourth centuries there was, for instance, a wide development of so-called 'minor orders'—door-keeper, exorcist, lector, acolyte. They grew up as what we can but call 'lay ministries' suited to their times. Naturally lay ministries, when exercised publicly and continuously, need some measure of ecclesiastical recognition: their 'order' must be seen in that light. But here again with the course of time these ministries came to be swallowed up into the presbyteral one. By the high middle ages the same fate, as regards the western church, had overtaken the diaconate. All became mere liturgical stepping stones to the priesthood.

The inherent need of a healthy church for non-presbyteral ministries was, however, again manifested by the emergence of religious orders—monks, friars and nuns—whose male members were at first seldom intended to be ordained, or— if they were—their type of ministry was viewed as strikingly different from that of the diocesan clergy. Here again, however, a levelling out process quickly began to take place— transferring certain 'religious' characteristics to the traditional clergy, but at the same time tending towards the ordination of all educated male religious. Modern pressures to obtain the ordination of teaching brothers may be viewed in this light.

Yet every time the pattern of a rather monolithic ministry has begun to emerge, new forces have appeared working in an opposite direction. The modern lay apostolate movement can be seen in this way: new ministries emerging almost spontaneously here and there, but at the same time an almost instant reaction to try somehow to 'discipline' this diversity: for instance, by allowing in a country a single 'Catholic Action' movement (not actually presbyteral, yet defined as a participation in the hierarchy's apostolate, which is a very presbyteral conception).

Vatican II has affirmed the existence of a variety of charisms and the necessity for a plurality of ministries.

Theology cannot state the concrete pattern these ministries should take at any particular moment, but it can state that they must not be conceived as all assimilable to the presbyterate either in the line of sacrament or in that of hierarchical direction. 'The laity must not be deprived of the possibility of acting on their own accord' (*Apostolicam Actuositatem*, a. 24): a statement which indicates no more than the basic condition for a variety of fruitful ministries in the church of God.

A third theme of particular significance today is that of 'segregation'. This too is one of vast dimensions, which can be hardly more than indicated here. Its proper understanding is fundamental for New Testament thought and life, though it may take on different verbal forms. Christian life involves a total separation from sin, from the world, from the unclean, from the flesh (Rm 6: 11–14; 7: 5–6; 8: 5–9; 12: 2; etc). This separation or segregation is accomplished essentially by baptism—the sign of God's call, and its acceptance by man in faith. This separation and entering into the heritage of Christ is truly a 'consecration', a making sacred or holy, and as a consequence christians can be called 'saints'. But this christian consecration is not a segregation from things or into places. Apart from withdrawal from activities held to be positively sinful, it has no sociological manifestation. There are not profane and sacred things, profane and sacred places: 'The earth is the Lord's and everything in it' (1 Cor 10: 26). 'There is nothing outside a man which can defile him' (Mk 7: 14); 'Neither on this mountain nor in Jerusalem ... but in spirit and in truth will you worship' (Jn 4: 21–3). 'What God has cleansed you must not call common' (Ac 9: 15). The problems of 1 Corinthians 8 and Romans 14 are just here: 'We are no worse off if we do not eat, and no better off if we do' (1 Cor 8: 8). Christian consecration and segregation do not involve opting out of some activities or restricting oneself to some places. Baptism makes sacred but it finds the sacred in the created in its wholeness.

Clearly there is a special moment in christian life which is in a unique way sacred and in which there was segregation from the start: the moment of the Lord's Supper. Christians were alone for that, and Paul's comparisons in 1 Corinthians 10 do suggest that he saw it as somehow the christian equivalent to Israelite and pagan sacred occasions. But it is clear that every christian is equally involved in this type of 'segregation' and its sacredness, and moreover that it somehow signs the potential sacredness of everything else and hence of the non-segregation of all the rest of christian life: 'Whatever you do, do all to the glory of God' (1 Cor 10:31).

This common theology is really basic for a sound understanding of the ministry because in so far as the christian ministry may involve a particular 'segregation', it still remains wholly of this theological type: a more intense concentration upon the gospel of God, but not a sociological separation. Paul himself is the very type of it. He is 'set apart for the gospel of God'—segregation—but he remains a tent-maker, earning his living by selling his wares or his labour to unbelievers. This is basic to the theology of the ministry. We cannot go here into the complicated story of subsequent centuries, in which the sacred came too often to be seen as a recognisable sphere of life separable from the profane, and then as a sphere of life properly belonging to the ordained rather than all christians;[1] in which too consecration for holiness came to be seen rather as ordination or religious profession than as baptism. All of which came

[1] In a curious way one can see how the same process has operated in the particular field of music. The original position was that all music is suitable for praising God: 'Praise him with blasts of the trumpet, praise him with lyre and harp, praise him with drums and dancing, praise him with strings and reeds, praise him with clashing symbols' (Ps 150). However, little by little the Catholic tradition instead sacralised the organ and excluded every other form of musical instrument from the church as being 'secular'.

gradually to establish an outlook according to which priest-hood was somehow incompatible with secular occupations. Such a view was never in fact fully implemented, but it has been constantly there in the background—from the time of St Cyprian at least, to our own day—to declare from time to time that certain non-sinful human activities were never-theless *per se* unsuitable for the priest. Theology must deny this, both on account of the New Testament evidence and from the intrinsic nature of the christian economy.

The Vatican II Decree on Presbyteral Ministry and Life stresses that the 'segregation' required of the priesthood (a. 3) is a strictly theological one, not sociological. Paul is taken as its explicit model. Hence the decree goes out of its way to commend both the worker priest and the married priest (a. 8 and 16). Pastoral reasons may justify a priest either working for his living with his own hands or not doing so, either being married or not being married, but the theological nature of the christian priesthood necessarily leaves such questions fully open.

The concept of a kind of sacredness of ordained ministers which requires from 'congruity' their segregation from various lawful human activities, including marriage, seems inextricably bound up with an implicit clericalisation of the Lord's Supper and a clericalisation too of the ideal of imitating Christ. It is not compatible with the New Testa-ment understanding of consecration and the holy.

If the nature of the ordained ministry in no way rules out any non-sinful human activity for the minister, there goes with this the implication that theology has in the end little to say about what proportion of a priest's time should be taken up by specifically ministerial functions, and equally how far he should be financially supported by the church. In all ages there have been many priests, and good priests, the greater part of whose working life has been given to what can be listed as 'secular' occupations—such as tent-making, agriculture, the school teaching of non-religious subjects, historical research. The general principle that the church should support its ministers depends in application upon the amount of time individual ministers give to explicit ministry, and the regulation of this depends again upon pastoral needs within a particular context, not on theology.

A fourth theme, already touched upon, is that of celibacy. It is scripturally and theologically certain that there is in the church a charism of celibacy which provides a special witness to the kingdom and which can also greatly contribute to the effectiveness of many ministries. It is verified by christian history that celibacy can be pastorally of great value, especially in the itinerant and missionary ministry. It is theologically certain that a church faithful to the New Testament must make room for and encourage the acceptance of this charism, and that while it can equally fittingly be embraced by the non-ordained (including women!) it is also fitting that among men commissioned for the episcopal and presbyteral ministries this charism be widely found.

However, it is also clear in principle, and can again be proved from christian experience, that the conjunction in a single person of the sacraments of orders and matrimony is not only theologically permissible but pastorally valuable. Unless principles are to be applied in this field seriously different from those acceptable elsewhere in theology, it is impossible to build up any strong relationship between the ministerial priesthood and celibacy. Canonical practice in the greater part of the church over a number of centuries can in no way be theologically decisive.

In this matter we have absolutely clear New Testament evidence. It is positive not negative guidance; moreover, it does not merely state facts but propounds what is suitable. Short of rejecting the Pastoral Epistles from the canon, theology can only accept the witness of 1 Timothy 3:2-5 and Titus 1:5-6. Here is a clear instance in which western Catholics, used to a particular ecclesiastical tradition, have to accept concretely Vatican II's message that the teaching office of the church 'is not above the word of God, but serves it' (*Dei Verbum*, a. 10). Furthermore, it is an historical fact —which theology cannot ignore—that there have been married Catholic priests carrying on a fruitful ministry in every single age of the church from the first to the twentieth century.

Theology, then, can only recognise the distinction between the charisms of the ordained ministry and that of celibacy. It must recognise that both the linking in an individual life of the priesthood with celibacy and its linking with marriage have been providential in the order of history, both have scriptural foundation, and both can be pastorally fruitful.

The fifth and final theme is that which has in fact come to the fore in each of the preceding ones. The ministry is for the sake of church and mission, not the church for the ministry. One cannot, for instance, first of all posit an abstract 'life and spirituality of priests' and then relate the conditions of the ministry to that life. The change in emphasis in the different drafts of Vatican II's decree on the presbyterate is striking. The early drafts had tried to do just that: to lay down the holiness and life of priests first. The final decree does the opposite. It starts with ministry. Ministry is service and service to someone; it is service, normally, within the context of a local church. The deepest nature of the New Testament ministry is just this: it is a *diakonia*, and the theological principle for its structuring is exactly that of relevance to the local fellowship and witness of the people of God in a particular space-time context.

Historically, this is more or less what has happened; but it is also true that certain patterns of ministry have, especially in later times, become too rigid and have been maintained even when seriously unadapted to the *diakonia* of the people of God in a particular context. Many examples, especially from missionary history, can prove this with complete objectivity.

The *diakonia* of the ordained ministry has to provide the core of word and sacrament for the church, and that includes a regular eucharistic celebration for every real local community of baptised faithful. Any pattern for the ordained ministry which in a particular historical-social context seriously fails to do this must be condemned theologically. At the same time the pattern of the ordained ministry has to be such as to stimulate rather than supplant a variety of other ministries in the church—missionary, prophetic and those relating to social service—so that the calling of the whole christian people and the diversity of charisms is assisted rather than suppressed, and the witness and communion of the whole church, local and catholic, effectively served in the changing world of history, geography and economics.

9

PROBLEMS OF THE MINISTRY IN
EASTERN AFRICA

I

In almost every part of the Catholic Church today there is
a great deal of discussion about the shape which the
ordained ministry ought to take. In part this is a theological
discussion, but it is also to a very large extent a sociological
one, dependent upon an analysis of the actual conditions of
the ministry, its recruitment, its apparent relevance to
modern conditions. In no part of the world is a discussion
of this kind more necessary than in Africa, where the church
is facing a major ministerial crisis which is developing
with unprecedented rapidity. Chapter vi of *Church and
Mission in Modern Africa* treated this subject at some
length, but in an effort to make the problem and possible
solutions to it clearer still, I return to it here with a more
precise analysis of the situation in three countries—Tanzania, Uganda and Zambia. The aim is to offer a careful
assessment of the number and distribution of priests at
national and diocesan levels as related to the Catholic
population and its growth in four years. It is largely based
on the statistical data provided in the two volumes of the
Catholic Directory of Eastern Africa, one for 1965, the other
for 1968–9. The former provides us with statistics for June
1963, the latter for June 1967. Doubtless the figures given
are far from entirely accurate, but they appear to be in
general reliable enough for the indication of trends and
the comparison of different types of situation. A few obvious

improbabilities are pointed out in the appropriate place. Three tables, worked out by me with the help of a calculating machine, contain the relevant information for the three countries.[1] It is a pity that for the three countries we have not at hand the statistics of any year later than 1967 but it should always be borne in mind that the population totals for 1970 are considerably higher.[2]

In each table column A gives the 1967 Catholic population of each diocese (this does not include catechumens; their number would usually add another 5 to 10% to the total). Column B puts the same as a percentage of the total population of the area. Column C lists the total growth in the number of Catholics in four years. D reshapes this as an absolute growth percentage over four years. Note that 3%, or slightly more, is roughly the annual general growth rate of population in these countries as a whole, so dioceses which have a growth in four years of not much more than 12% are claiming little increase beyond that of the newly baptised children of existing church members. Column E gives the number of priests in 1967 while F indicates the difference between this and the 1963 figures.[3] Finally column G shows the 1967 ratio between priests and Catholics.

[1] Figures for seminarians given in the body of the text are not taken from the Directories but from the very carefully edited *Status Seminariorum Indigenarum*, published annually by Propaganda Fide, Rome. The figures for 'Seminarians Theologians' provided in the 1968–9 *Directory* are in fact unreliable. They include at least two major mistakes. Firstly, the title 'Seminarians Theologians' is ambiguous and has caused confusion. Was it meant to exclude 'philosophers'? As far as I can see all the countries included the latter except for Tanzania. This means that if the column really means 'Major seminarians' then the Tanzanian figure is more than a 100 lower than it should be. Secondly, the figure for Uganda includes under the diocese of Gulu all the refugee Sudanese seminarians at present studying at Lakor. This has put the Ugandan figure about 100 higher than it should be.

[2] For Zambia the 1969 figures are available and I include some for comparison.

[3] It is probable that in counting up the number of priests some dioceses include and some exclude priests on long leave; indeed, the same diocese may well vary its practice from year to year; hence

It is worth noting that in general in Africa the numbers the church claims as members are smaller than the numbers who appear as such in a government census, although the discrepancy is not as great with Catholics as with Protestants. That is to say, the churches have a large fringe community which are not included in their own statistics, but who nevertheless consider themselves to belong.[4]

Some people ask, why be so concerned with numbers and statistics? One might reply with the words of Churchill: 'Great numbers are at least an explanation of great changes.' The Catholic Church is not, and has never seen herself as, an elitist group, a sect. If she accepts vast numbers of baptised members, and indeed goes out to get them, then she has the responsibility of providing a ministry adequate to them, a structured church community life in which to participate. In the age of the population explosion this inevitably creates fresh problems, but these problems cannot even be assessed without a careful consideration of statistics. To despise the latter and talk of concentrating on quality instead, is either to deny the real nature of the Catholic communion or to bury one's head in the sand. While to go on saying 'Deus providebit' is essentially an un-christian, because an anti-incarnational, attitude. God provides across the brains and resourcefulness of man. That resourcefulness must, I believe, enable us to carry through without delay a major structural revolution without which the quickly growing churches of Africa can only crumble into chaos.

II
TANZANIA[5]

The Catholic Church on the mainland of Tanzania has recently celebrated its centenary, commemorating the found-

some of the more startling discrepancies may well depend in part upon a difference of practice in those compiling the diocesan statistics.

[4] See T. Beetham, *Christianity and the New Africa*, Appendix I, pp. 163–164.

[5] Zanzibar was not included in the 1963 Directory figures, and I

ing of Bagamoyo mission by Father Horner of the Congregation of the Holy Ghost in March 1868. The White Fathers started their work in the western half of the country ten years later. Their first caravan set out from Bagamoyo for Tabora in June 1878. Ten years on again the Benedictines of the Congregation of St Ottilien were beginning to evangelise in the southern regions. Of course, in many of the twenty-two dioceses that exist today the first work dates from a much later period, well after the first world war.

In the country as a whole Catholics today form about 18% of the population, and their own annual growth rate would seem to be about 6%. For the preceding four years, 1959–63, the annual growth rate must have been higher, around 8%. It will probably continue to fall and by 1971 may be no more than 5%. In the country as a whole there has been a small increase in priests in the last four years. This increase has been wholly among local priests—now over 400 strong. The latter are reinforced by about 25 a year. On the other hand during the last two years the total of expatriate priests has actually decreased and in the next four years this tendency will certainly be accentuated. Most missionary societies have ordinations today hardly half as big as those of ten years ago. Moreover the average age of missionaries in many Tanzanian dioceses is high, which means that the casualty rate in the next years is likely to be high too. By 1971 there may be over 500 Tanzanian priests, but the expatriates (in 1967: 876) may well be down to about 800.

Evidently a decrease in foreign personnel and an increase in local personnel is wholly advantageous. The quicker the majority of priests working in Tanzania are Tanzanians the better and this may well be the case in less than ten years time. Nevertheless the two processes together are hardly doing more than keep the total number of priests fairly

---

have excluded it from the 1967 ones and from consideration here. It has, in fact, some 4,000 Catholics and four priests.

constant while the Catholic population is rapidly increasing. Hence the national priest: Catholic ratio is growing
steadily worse. In 1959 it was 1:1,235; in 1963 it was
1:1,460.[6] By 1967 it was 1:1,745. A worsening of over 500
in eight years is certainly serious, and the rate of its increase
is itself growing. One will be lucky if the ratio is not well
over 1:2,000 by 1971.

It must also be noted that the increase of Tanzanians
and the decrease of expatriates do not take place in the
same dioceses. Some of those which are hit hardest by the
decrease in expatriates hardly gain at all from the increase
in Tanzanians.

Turning from general considerations regarding the
country as a whole, we can see that from a church point of
view Tanzania may be divided into three sections, the Catholic population being by no means evenly distributed and
uniform. First of all, there are areas in which Catholics form
well over 30% of the total population. These areas are
four: (a) a large central-southern area including Peramiho,
Iringa and Mahenge; (b) the North-West—Bukoba and
Rulenge; (c) the remote south-western diocese of Karema:
the district of Ufipa which is the most predominantly Catholic part of the whole country; (d) the small but highly
populated diocese of Moshi on the slopes of Kilimanjaro.
These seven dioceses have between them well over half the
Catholics of the country and 60% of the African priests,
but five of them are the five dioceses with the worst priest:
faithful ratio (over 1:2,300).

Secondly, there is the group of dioceses, covering roughly
the whole central part of Tanzania, in which Catholics are
over 10% and under 25%. These run from Kigoma in the
west to Morogoro in the east, from Musoma in the north
to Nachingwea in the south. They are again seven. Their
character varies from that of Morogoro, an old-established
diocese with a fairly high percentage in population but a

[6] See F. Murray, *African Ecclesiastical Review*, October 1965, 347.

very low growth rate, to Kigoma, a young diocese with far fewer Catholics but a far higher growth rate. Thus Morogoro is linked with our first groups of dioceses while Kigoma comes close to the third.

This third group consists of eight dioceses with under 10%. These are the chief areas of pioneer missionary work. The number of their Catholics is low but their growth rate is mostly pretty high. They fall into two groups. The first covers the coastal areas with their strong Moslem population. The second is the middle north—Arusha, Mbulu and Shinyanga—where the great bulk of the population is still neither Christian nor Moslem. It is a large area where extensive evangelisation began rather late; it was for long somehow neglected between the Holy Ghost Fathers' concentration to the east of it and the White Fathers' concentration in the west. The diocese of Mwanza could almost be included in this sub-group though, strictly, it belongs to the second division. Finally, Mbeya has also less than 10%, but it stands on its own in a number of ways. It is a largely christian area with strong Moravian, Lutheran and Anglican communities, and the Catholic growth rate is comparatively low.

To turn in greater detail to some individual dioceses: Mwanza is an old established diocese in an area of high population but conversions in the early years were extremely slow. The Sukuma people do not seem very susceptible to organised religion. Recently, however, there has been a certain improvement with the result that Catholics have increased by 23,000 in four years. At the same time there are twelve priests fewer than in 1963. Such a situation is undoubtedly disturbing.

Kigoma is still more serious. It is an area of young mission with a very rapid increase in the Catholic population. A very high growth rate and a decrease of six priests in four years is grave indeed. Kigoma has only two Tanzanian priests and very few major seminarists. What are those responsible going to do in such cases?

A first answer to this question might be to send priests from those dioceses which have an increase in priests such as Moshi, Bukoba and Peramiho. These are the strongest areas of catholicism in the country and their priests should

Table 1. *The Catholic Church in Tanzania*

Diocese	A Catholic popula- tion 1967	B % of total popula- tion	C Increase in 4 years (1963–7)	D Absolute growth % over 4 years	E Priests 1967	F Increase or decrease in 4 years	G Priest: faithful ratio 1967
Arusha	9,000	2·5	3,600	66·6	23	+8	1: 391
Bukoba*	213,326	50	32,398	17·9	92	+9	2319
D'Salaam	44,649	7	18,374	69·9	44	+4	1014
Dodoma	101,051	14	23,485	30·2	52	+8	1943
Iringa	198,677	33	54,631	37·9	76	+6	2614
Karema†	207,816	77	19,396	10·2	84	+4	2474
Kigoma	68,163	14	21,958	47·5	39	−6	1747
Mahenge	85,581	61	8,561	11·1	57	−5	1501
Mbeya	55,574	8	8,439	17·9	53	+7	1049
Mbulu	51,829	9	12,448	31·6	33		1570
Morogoro	167,183	24	16,869	11·2	87	−8	1921
Moshi	241,464	48	58,421	31·9	75	+15	3219
Musoma	91,569	20	25,957	39·5	44		2081
Mwanza	109,906	10	22,913	26·3	76	−12	1446
Nachingwea	33,994	12	5,109	17·6	20		1699
Ndanda	51,358	9	13,747	36·5	66	+6	778
Peramiho‡	257,463	56	40,794	18·8	147	+20	1751
Rulenge	92,590	34	17,663	23·5	33		2805
Same	13,006	9	4,233	48·2	18	+6	722
Shinyanga	36,070	5	11,170	44·8	43	+3	838
Tabora	60,519	10	19,134	46·2	77	−1	785
Tanga	34,276	5	3,750	12·2	34	+3	1008
Total	2,225,064	19	443,150	24·8	1273	+67	1747

* I give the Bukoba figures as they are to be found in the *Directory*, but they seem to be seriously incorrect. Where the *Catholic Directory* gives a total population of 421,280 for 1967, the government census of the same year gives the figure of 383,165, a difference of 38,315. The census figure is surely the more reliable. Probably the *Directory* figure for Catholics—213,326—is similarly inflated. It has been suggested to me by a missionary on the spot that the 1967 priest:faithful ratio for Bukoba was probably in the region of 1:2,083 or even lower.

† Now renamed Sumbawanga.

‡ Peramiho is now divided into Songea and Njombe.

be willing to strengthen the weaker dioceses. But when one turns to Moshi one finds the worst priest: people ratio in the whole country: 1 : 3,219. In such circumstances it seems unreasonable to think of sending priests from Moshi elsewhere. Peramiho is in rather better state and is in fact already being called upon, but even there the increase of 20 priests in four years has been balanced by one of over 40,000 faithful.

Dar es Salaam is another serious case. It has the highest growth rate in the country, not on account of conversions but because of the influx of people into the capital. Though the ratio is not bad at present, particular care needs to be devoted to the one large city in the whole country and the priests in the archdiocese will certainly need to be further reinforced in the near future.

Moshi is another case again. Despite the fact that it has some 50 Tanzanian priests and a fair number of major seminarists, its pastoral position is extremely serious. It is, of course, helped by its small area and high density of population. At the other extreme from this is Tabora whose priest: faithful ratio is in theory a good one. Nevertheless Tabora is a vast area with a very low density of population and bad communications. With a rather elderly clergy, its condition is none too sound even with its present low ratio.

It is, in fact, hardly possible to point to a single diocese whose present state is fully sound or future prospects evidently bright, though Bukoba (58 local priests), Peramiho (53 local priests) and Karema (43 local priests) are undoubtedly in the strongest position. But even they are in no position to offer the really extensive help to their neighbours which is needed.

This analysis makes clear that the church in Tanzania is already entering upon a major crisis and all the signs are that its proportions will become worse in the coming years. This is true despite the fact that Tanzania has been favoured until now with a larger Catholic missionary force than any African country of comparable size (except the

Congo), and has what is relatively an excellent record on local priest training.

There are three types of general need today with regard to the supply of priests. The first is to provide an increasing number of extra qualified Tanzanian priests for posts in the teaching world of secondary school, seminary and university, for administrative positions, for town parishes. The second is to maintain the momentum of evangelisation in areas such as Arusha and Kigoma where it is still in its early stages. The third is to provide adequate pastoral care and the administration of the sacraments for the millions of existing Catholics in the rural areas.

It is the first of these three that is being most seriously faced today. A large proportion of recently ordained priests are being sent for further studies to qualify them for specialised tasks. This is absolutely right but it is to be noted that it means that relatively few young priests are made available for basic pastoral and missionary work. It is these two vast fields which require radically new consideration if the life of the church, which remains, and will remain, predominantly in the rural areas, is not simply to fall to pieces. It is to be noted that the pastoral situation has, in fact, already begun to deteriorate considerably. Evidence of this is to be found, *inter alia*, in the very serious decline in the number of church marriages which is steadily continuing. It is absolutely certain that neither the missionary societies nor the present local system of ministry and ministerial training can provide for these needs.

III
UGANDA

The Catholic Church in Uganda is now ninety years old. It began when Father Lourdel and Brother Amans landed at Entebbe in February 1879, though in many parts of the country missionary work only started very much later—in the northern regions, with the arrival of the Verona Fathers, after 1910. In 1970 it includes twelve dioceses and more than three million Catholics. The majority of its bishops are Ugandans and they are assisted by some 300 local priests, 1,300 local sisters and nearly 200 local brothers. The church in Uganda is well-known for the brilliance of its beginning with the rapid conversion of twenty-two future canonised saints and their companions, for its swift progress in many fields in the subsequent decades, for the fact that it received the first Catholic African bishop of modern times. Uganda is today a predominantly christian country, and Pope Paul's historic visit in July 1969 is a recognition of all that has been accomplished.

It may be noted first that Uganda is a far smaller country than Tanzania and, on the whole, a far more densely populated one. A rather close population certainly makes rapid growth in church numbers easier. The very scale of the quantitative growth of the church in Uganda, especially during the last twenty years, has however created a situation today which cannot honestly be described otherwise than as one of crisis: in some ways more serious than that of almost any other country in central Africa other than the Sudan.

As regards the statistics, the erection of certain dioceses, together with the reshaping of the Kampala-Jinja dioceses since 1963 force one to couple Fort Portal with Hoima, Gulu with Moroto, Jinja with Kampala, and Kabale with Mbarara for certain of the data. The transfer of the so-called 'Lost Counties' area (the parishes of Mugalike, Bujuni and Bukuumi) after 1963 from what is now the archdiocese of Kampala to the diocese of Hoima creates a still more awkward problem for the comparison of statistics. I have resolved it by subtracting the Catholic population involved (some 37,000) and the number of priests (9) from the 1963 Kampala (then called Rubaga) figures and adding it to the Fort Portal-Hoima total for 1963. (If I had not done so, the Fort Portal-Hoima increase for four years would stand at 80,000: a quite misleading figure.)

In general the figures provided by the Directory seem fairly reliable, though the increases claimed for Gulu and Moroto are so large as to make one wonder whether they can be really accurate (especially in view of the relatively small number of catechumens listed); on the other hand, I suspect that the figures for Tororo may be too low. As a whole and with these qualifications, there seems no reason to question the substantial reliability of the picture these statistics present.

The picture of the country as a whole is one of a most rapidly increasing Catholic population. The 1967 figure of 2,800,000 Catholics form 37% of the population and nowhere do they fall below 20%. The annual growth rate for the four years 1963-7 must be a good 7%. This will actually be an increase on the preceding four years which had an annual rate of something like 6%. Whereas in Tanzania the annual growth rate seems to be declining, here it has actually gone up, and this despite the fact that the body of priests working in the country is far less numerous.

One may well ask why the trend at present is the reverse of Tanzania's, and further research will be needed to give an adequate answer. (Especially as Uganda claims a smaller number of catechumens than Tanzania.) It may well be connected with the fact that there is no large scale alternative to christianity in Uganda—the Moslem community is small in comparison with that of Tanzania and limited to certain parts of the country. Equally, there are only two christian communions of any size—the Catholic and the Anglican—and the Catholics have at present a far larger number of ministers in the field. Independent African churches have hitherto made little lasting impact. Again there is no tribal group of any size in Uganda which has remained so considerably impervious to the attractions of any world religion as have, for example, the Sukuma and the Masai in Tanzania. Sociologically, in Uganda today there seems to exist a very extensive desire to join a large-scale religion and there is very little choice within the country. In other countries there is less desire and more choice. Consequently, it seems likely that the nominally Catholic proportion of the population will continue to increase rapidly in the coming years. By 1980 there may be well over five million people listed as Catholics.

The position with regard to priests is a very different one. As our table shows, there has been an increase of 104 in four years. Over half of this is an increase in local priests, but there has also been some continued increase in ordained expatriates mainly in the north (unlike Tanzania). It is, however, more than probable that for the next four years a decrease in the foreign missionaries will have to be noted. The increase in African priests, on the other hand, has of late been much slower than that in Tanzania. Uganda used to have more local priests than Tanzania. It was overtaken in 1957 and now has far fewer.

	Tanzania	Uganda
1957	186	184
1967	401	279

Furthermore the number of major seminarians in Uganda is also smaller, and was, in fact, until 1969 steadily declining. The figures are as follows:[7]

	Tanzania	Uganda
1965	279	199
1966	298	176
1967	294	162
1968	284	145
1969	288	194

Hence there is no prospect of any very startling increase in the number of local ordinations, at least for the next five years, rather the contrary. The large 1969 intake has been followed by a still bigger 1970 one. However, the numbers leaving the seminary are also increasing. Though the

[7] The date these figures are valid for is April 15 of each year. The figures include those studying in Rome.

5

ordinations from 1974 on will probably be bigger, they are unlikely to be phenomenally so.

Quite apart from the future, however, the present ministerial position of Uganda is about the worst in the whole of Africa. Fr Masson SJ, in the *Nouvelle Revue Théologique* of March 1963 (p. 284), already pointed out the particular seriousness of Uganda's position. He then gave it a priest: people ratio of 1 : 2950. In AFER of October 1965 (p. 347) Fr F. Murray, commenting on the 1963 ratio of 1 : 3,000, spoke of Uganda's 'alarming figure'. In AFER of April 1966 I myself indicated that Uganda's ratio had now reached 1 : 3,333 and continued: 'Notice how bad Uganda's position is despite having been for long the most forward country from the viewpoint of native vocations'. Little notice seems to have been taken of these warnings. By 1967 there was just one priest for every 3,470 Catholics in Uganda (compare Tanzania's 1 : 1,747). The situation of Uganda can only be described from this point of view as catastrophic. It is already almost on a par with quite a number of the least provided South American countries, and it is getting rather rapidly worse year by year. The inevitable consequence is a steady reduction in the proportion of the number of Catholics who are practising and a decrease in the number of communions and of church marriages. A condition is built up in which a state of non-practising becomes ever more normal.

Turning to some individual dioceses, it is to be noted that the diversity of situation in Uganda is far less than that in Tanzania. The diocesan percentages of the general population here vary from 65% in Masaka to 21% in Jinja (as against Tanzania's range from 77% in Karema to 2·5% in Arusha). This is, in fact, a general characteristic of Uganda, being far smaller and more homogeneous. The chief contrast within the church remains one between the two Buganda dioceses and the rest.

It is striking how even Kampala, with its old tradition of a local clergy, has a worse priest: people ratio than any dio-

Table 2. *The Catholic Church in Uganda*

Diocese	A Catholic population 1967	B % of total population	C Increase in 4 years (1963–7)	D Absolute growth % over 4 years	E Priests 1967	F Increase or decrease in 4 years	G Priest: faithful ratio 1967
Arua	308,092	58	55,788	22	70	+4	1:4401
F/Portal Hoima	121,990 90,031	32 36	42,723	25	49 24	+15	2490 3751
Gulu (+Lira) Moroto	323,871 55,892	42 25	149,658	65	86 26	+39	3766 2150
Jinja Kampala	164,250 569,292	21 42	188,692	35	35 194	+14	4693 2934
Kabale Mbarara	209,214 229,116	32 34	122,669	39	40 61	+19	5230 3756
Masaka	281,029	65	50,725	22	107	+6	2626
Tororo	457,570	30	55,760	14	118	+7	3878
Total	2,810,347	37	666,943	31	810	+104	3470

cese in Tanzania, save only Moshi. The worst situation of any diocese in the country is Kabale with the almost unbelievable ratio of 1 : 5,225. This is a consequence, of course, of a very intense conversion movement both there and in Mbarara during the last twelve years or so. It is well known how vital is christian life at present in Kabale, but there can be little hope for the sound development of a structured church community in the area unless both additional immediate help is given and new systems of ministry are recognised to cater for a type of situation which the Catholic Church has almost never until recently had to face elsewhere. What is true of Kabale is largely true also of Jinja, Mbarara, Arua, Tororo, Hoima and Lira.

The church in Uganda has an absolute duty to face up

to three areas of fact within the field of ministry, all of
which have hitherto been more or less ignored. The first is
that for the whole country there is a quite exceptional
shortage of priests. This is a fairly new problem: the result
of the enormous increase in the numbers of the faithful in
the post-war years. It did not exist prior to 1940, when the
prospects of local recruitment of the traditional type anyway seemed more encouraging. The Church has gone on
complacently sunning itself in the light of the pre-war
record.

The second area of fact concerns geographical distribution. The local priests who do exist are massed in just two
out of the twelve dioceses. Of the 279 Ugandan priests listed
in 1967, no less than 175 belong to Kampala and Masaka,
the other hundred being shared between ten dioceses. The
most poorly provided region, from this point of view, is the
East and North-East. The five dioceses of Gulu, Lira,
Moroto, Tororo and Jinja have between them over one
million Catholics but just 39 Ugandan priests. It is clear
that collegiality would mean very little if this situation
could not be rectified, and it is certainly to other dioceses
in Uganda rather than abroad that Baganda priests should
be looking for service in this juncture.

The third point is that the existing inadequate ordained
personnel is too often misplaced not only geographically
but also functionally. Thus the multiplication of minor
seminaries for each diocese (and even more than one per
diocese) with often large priest staffs has resulted in some
10% of all priests being now engaged as full-time seminary
teachers. And these are mostly chosen from among younger
priests. Very possibly no other country in the world has so
large a proportion of its priesthood tied up in minor seminaries, and to such comparatively little effect—as the annual
figures prove.

The church in Uganda still has great possibilities: not
only an extraordinary numerical growth, but a truly indigenous christian life deeply rooted in some areas, the

much appreciated tradition of the martyrs, the flexibility potentially present in what is still a young church. But there is no country in Africa today where reluctance to face up to the inadequacies of the established system and the need for re-orientation is beginning to have more disastrous effect upon the whole quality of the church's life.

IV
ZAMBIA

Whereas the history of the church in Tanzania goes back to the late 1860s and that of the church in Uganda to the late 1870s, Catholic missionary effort in modern Zambia only dates from the 1890s. This late start makes a considerable difference. Nor was a great deal done even when a beginning had been made. The expansion during the next twenty years, except for White Father activity in the far north, was rather slight. By 1920 there were still only thirteen mission stations in the whole country as against forty-nine in Uganda. Catholic missionaries—Capuchins and Franciscan Conventuals—only began work in most of the west of the country (the present dioceses of Livingstone, Ndola and Solwezi) after 1930. Today's diocese of Monze still had a single mission station—Chikuni—in 1949. The first Zambian Catholic priest was ordained in 1939 and a regular succession of ordinations only began in the mid-forties (Uganda's first priest was ordained in 1913, Tanzania's in 1917). All this has to be borne in mind if any comparison is made between the state of the church in one country and another.

The whole character of Zambia must also be remembered. On one side, an area more than three-quarters the size of Tanzania (and three times bigger than Uganda); on the other, a population only one-third the size of Tanzania's—and the latter is itself a sparsely populated country. The general very low density of population here has certainly made missionary work more difficult, especially with a relatively small missionary force. The situation has now been greatly complicated by the development on the copperbelt of the largest industrial area in eastern Africa. Its population today is not far off a million: that is to say nearly one quarter of Zambia's total is concentrated in a radius of forty miles round Kitwe.

Certainly in total numbers the church in Zambia—claiming 647,640 in 1967 (728,961 in 1969)—is much smaller than those of Uganda and Tanzania, though it does represent about the same proportion of the general population as that of Tanzania: 17 or 18%. It has also in the past been growing somewhat less fast. (High rates of growth tend to go with the more dense population areas; and this makes one query the very high rate claimed for Livingstone, a particularly sparsely populated diocese.) The 1963–7 general annual growth rate would seem to be a little over 5%. This may be a slight increase on the preceding four years and the 1969 figures indicate a further rise in the growth rate to over 6%. This may be related to the present rapid increase in educational facilities.

It may be noted here that the islamic alternative to christianity hardly exists for Zambians, though there does exist—far more than in Uganda and Tanzania—a very wide variety both of mission-based Protestant churches and African independent churches. In Mufulira eleven churches of different communions stand side by side in a single street.

The total number of priests in the country rose by fifty-five in four years, but it should be noted that the increase is almost entirely in expatriates. There has been only a handful of local ordinations. The total number of local Zambian priests in 1967 stood at fifty with twenty-two major seminarians (the 1969 figure is twenty-one). Zambia may be lucky to have been able to continue increasing its team of foreign priests in years when some countries are already suffering an actual decrease, and it is of course—in the absence of local priests—much needed. The 1969 figures show that the growth of foreign priests by about twelve a year is still going on, but it is doubtful whether it

can continue much longer; whether it does or not, the extremely small number of major seminarians augurs ill for
the future. Nevertheless, at present the priest: faithful ratio
(1 : 1,611) remains somewhat better than that of Tanzania
and far better than that of Uganda (this is characteristic of
an earlier stage in missionary development).

This last, of course, refers only to the general priest:
faithful ratio. If we take that of local priests to faithful we
get a very different picture:[8]

Tanzania	1 : 5,557
Uganda	1 : 10,431
Zambia	1 : 12,950

Yet even in regard to local priests the situation is rather
less catastrophic than that of the five dioceses of Eastern
Uganda (Gulu, Lira, Moroto, Tororo, Jinja):

1967	Catholics	local priests
Eastern Uganda	1,002,000	39
Zambia	648,000	50

In Zambia too, however, what local priests do exist are
concentrated in one area: the old White Father territory
of the North-East. If one considers the position as regards
Zambian priests in the five dioceses of the centre and west
of the country, one gets the following bleak information:[9]

Livingstone	0
Lusaka	5
Monze	1
Ndola	6
Solwezi	1

Turning to individual dioceses, the first thing that strikes
one is the rather low annual growth rate in some of the
country parts where the church is best established, notably
Mansa and Mbala. The explanation of this lies chiefly in

[8] The ratio for Malawi is 1 : 9,411; that for Kenya 1 : 18,944.
[9] The Directory gives 0 for Solwezi, but that was a mistake.

Table 3.   *The Catholic Church in Zambia*

Diocese	A Catholic popula- tion 1967	B % of total popula- tion*	C Increase in 4 years (1963–7)	D Absolute growth % over 4 years	E Priests, 1967	F Increase or decrease in 4 years†	G Priest: faithful ratio 1967
Chipata	78,105	15	12,422	18·9	46	−3	1:1698
Kasama	145,947	37	27,001	22·7	58	+3	2516
Livingstone	44,192	9	16,516	59·6	39	+6	1133
Lusaka	62,572	15	16,772	36·6	52	+9	1203
Mansa	92,104	24	9,567	11·5	54	+6	1706
Mbala	61,926	17	8,304	15·4	54	+12	1147
Monze	38,200	8	5,500	16·8	46	+15	830
Ndola	122,265	19	15,872	14·9	42	+4	2911
Solwezi	2,329	2	627	36·8	11	+3	212
Total	647,640	17	112,581	21·0	402	+55	1611

* The 1969 census has revealed that the general population of northern Zambia is less than was previous estimated. Hence the percentages here given on a 1967 basis are not very accurate. In particular the Catholic population of Kasama is well over 50%.

† The 1969 church figures show Chipata up 4 and Mbala down 2 in the number of priests. Some of these fluctuations in the figures have little real significance.

the extensive emigration of people from these country areas to the copperbelt, which is indeed being filled up above all with young people from Mansa, Kasama and Mbala. The 1969 census has revealed an actual decrease of population in the northern areas over the last six years.

The capital, Lusaka, has, like the copperbelt, grown rapidly these last years and in fact throughout Zambia the population is tending to concentrate along the line of rail. This fully accounts for the high growth rate of Lusaka archdiocese, indeed it should be a good deal larger still. After this, it is all the more bewildering to find Ndola diocese, which includes the whole of the copperbelt, claiming a growth rate which would seem to be less than 4% a year. Clearly something is very wrong here. The first National Development Plan (July 1966) estimated that the urban population was increasing by 8% a year between 1963 and 1967 (p. 284), while the 1969 census has shown that the copperbelt population did in fact grow in six years by almost 50%. It is impossible that the Catholic growth rate should be less than half the general one. Thus, to compare the Mbala and Ndola dioceses, in six years the total population of the former has actually decreased but its Catholic population has increased by about 23%. In Ndola the general population has grown by 50% but the diocese claims that the Catholic population has only grown by about 21%: obviously correct figures would indicate a Catholic growth in Ndola over the last six years of at least 70%. This is, indeed, a unique situation for an ostensibly missionary diocese. The explanation must lie in a pastoral condition of near breakdown. Even with the existing figures, Ndola has easily the worst priest: faithful ratio in the country (1 : 2,911). It is amazing that, though it is here the population of Zambia has been more and more accumulating in these years, only four of the fifty-five extra priests who arrived in these years were for Ndola. There are also very few catechists in this diocese—which is true of most African urban areas. It appears to be the case that in these circumstances the Catholic population simply cannot be properly assessed or, indeed, what is much more important—tended. A total of 200,000 and a ratio of 1 : 5,000 would be nearer the truth. It is worth reminding ourselves here that in many parts of Africa the 1970s are going to witness a process of urbanisation comparable with that of the copperbelt; as things stand at present they are likely equally to witness a complete urban breakdown of the church.

The Jesuit diocese of Monze is a young one with a fairly small number of christians and consequently a low theoretical priest: faithful ratio (1 : 830). But it has to be noted that this is particularly theoretical as over half the priests are not normally in pastoral work, the diocese having very extensive educational commitments. Its real pastoral ratio is probably about 1 : 2,000.

This analysis of the situation of the ministry in Zambia brings out three fundamental desiderata. The first is a territorial redeployment. The church has hitherto taken almost no notice of the massive shift of population to the towns and the fact that the copperbelt and Lusaka present a quite special situation. The old division of dioceses according to religious orders is here proving particularly harmful. This is a national responsibility and must be tackled nationally. Not to do so is both unreasonable and effectively disastrous for the church throughout the country. The arrival of the White Fathers at Mufulira is a small beginning in this regard.

The second relates to the remote countryside. Zambia, in common with Tanzania, has a countryside of vast area and very low population. Away from the copperbelt and the line of rail there can be few countries in Africa (excluding the areas of the Sahara and the Kalahari) with a generally lower population per square mile. Dioceses like Mbala and Livingstone, many hundreds of miles in length, put the problem of how to create a viable local church in rural Africa at its most acute. A new structural system is needed. The number of christians may not be enormous (Mbala's ratio is 1:1,147) but the sheer burden of mileage on bad bush roads for priests in central stations, and their resultant rare presence in many a remote outstation is something which can stifle the life of the church as effectively as the weight of overwhelming numbers in some other areas.

The third need (related to both the other two) is for an urgent reshaping and extension of the locally recruited ministry. Serious as is the situation in Uganda and Tanzania, they have nevertheless as a whole a comparatively numerous local clergy and a fair number of annual ordinations. For whatever reason Zambia is in a very different position. 34% of Uganda's priests are local men and 31% of Tanzania's, but only 12.5% of Zambia's. This helps give an extremely foreign impression to the Catholic Church in Zambia. And there seems next to no prospect of this improving with the present system; the number of seminarians remains extremely low, and even the total number of local sisters in 1967 was only 131, and in 1969 163. The removal of foreign missionaries here could consequently have far more devastating results than in the other two countries. It may not be imminent but one cannot base the church's future on the assumption that this will never happen.

V

In my *Church and Mission in Modern Africa* (pp. 209–10) I wrote that 'missionary societies seem almost everywhere to be feeling a pinch in vocations' and consequently that 'no increase in the missionary army comparable with that of the 1950s can be looked for'. I wrote this in 1966. Today I realise that it was a gross understatement. The diminution in missionary vocations is not now a pinch but a plunge, and it is affecting almost every single missionary sending country. Three years ago countries like Ireland still seemed rather little touched by this. Today it is not so. Planning within the young churches must take this fully to heart: the next years are bound to witness a very serious decline in the numbers of European and North American priests, brothers and sisters working in Africa. It would be quite irresponsible to close one's eyes to this fact. In the 1960s African dioceses could reasonably appeal abroad for large-scale help. In the 1970s they will not be able to do so.

It seems to me difficult to exaggerate the seriousness of the situation facing the church in most African countries today in this line of ministry. The preceding studies have attempted to analyse this situation in three different countries and a large number of varying dioceses. Taking the sixty or so dioceses existing in the five countries of Eastern Africa today (Kenya, Malawi, Tanzania, Uganda, Zambia) one can say that only about six of these could possibly stand upon their own feet with the present ministerial system and without massive foreign help now or for very many years to come. Those six are Masaka, Kampala, Bukoba, Peramiho, Moshi and Karema. Between them they have 378 of the 873 African priests in the five countries, and they have 225 of the 582 major seminarians: that is to say they have an average of sixty-three local priests and thirty-seven seminarians each. The other fifty-four dioceses have an average of nine local priests and less than seven seminarians each. Less than seven seminarians means that they cannot on an average expect anything like one new priest a year, considering the high drop-out rate in seminaries these days.

Furthermore, it is clear that even those six dioceses cannot possibly offer extensive help to the other fifty-four. Several of them—notably Kampala and Moshi—already have extremely bad priest: people ratios; moreover these same dioceses are still making use of considerable foreign help themselves.

Among the other fifty-four dioceses there are various sorts. There are some where development has been a matter of the last twenty years such as Monze (Zambia), Kitui (Kenya) and Mzuzu (Malawi), which are still in a relatively early and confident stage of mission work with a rather young average age for missionary personnel. There are dioceses (the majority) where this has been passed, where local vocations are not maturing in anything like adequate numbers, where difficulties are growing every year, but where a real state of crisis in ministry has not yet been reached. There are finally a group of dioceses such as Kabale (Uganda), Kisii (Kenya), Dedza (Malawi), Ndola (Zambia), which are already in a state of major crisis, even if they don't fully realise it. Their priest: people ratio is generally over the 1 : 4,000 mark. This last group is going to grow very rapidly in the coming years and indeed in some ways even so developed a diocese as Kampala could already be placed within this category.

In all these countries a rather high proportion of young ordained African priests are sent for further studies either at home or abroad and are then given more specialised assignments: teaching in secondary schools, teacher training colleges, minor and major seminaries; diocesan administration, the national secretariat, etc. A relatively small proportion of younger priests remain for long in 'bush work'. In many places this tends to be true as well of young missionaries.

Yet the fact remains that the vast majority of people in these countries live in completely rural surroundings and will continue to do so in the foreseeable future (Zambia alone can be an exception to this). Our pastoral system, even as we have had it until now and despite the undoubted primary concern most missionaries have had for the rural areas, has never been able to provide many of our people with the possibility of the sacraments more than once in two months, or worse. In very many dioceses the number of outstations attached to each mission, the distances involved, the bad roads, especially in the rainy season, have combined to make it quite impossible for the majority of christians in the more remote places to acquire any real sense of belonging to a local eucharistic community. The number of the baptised increases steeply year by year; at the same time there are fewer priests in the rural parishes—many missions which used to be staffed by three men now have two, and so on; some missions are even being closed and more will have to be soon; and the average age of priests in rural work is getting rather old, in some places terrifyingly so. It is next to impossible for older men to undertake the regular exhausting safaris involved in serving a mission which is really some fifteen distinct parishes.

Both the rural ministry in all five countries and the urban ministry in large built-up areas such as the copperbelt and Greater Kampala are approaching a situation of near breakdown for which the present system of ministry and of recruitment to the ministry offers absolutely no possibility of solution. The only conceivable solution lies in the courageous development of new patterns of ministry more adapted to social realities, and therefore more intrinsically African, than the present pattern which has been imported almost unchanged from western Europe, and from a Europe which is also not that of today. The present type of priest with his long training, full-time commitment, relatively high rates of pay or (at least) standard of living, and the freedom of celibacy will remain necessary, but it is absolutely clear that with this kind of priest alone we cannot maintain even a minimum of local pastoral service and sacramental life in the great majority of our dioceses, let alone achieve any sort of missionary dynamism among the millions of the unevangelised.

The introduction of a married diaconate is no adequate solution here. The diaconate is either a formalisation of lay ministry or it is a ministry auxiliary to the presbyterate within a local context. In neither case can it replace the presbyterate, and it is the latter which is effectively lacking here. As a stage in the evolution of the organised ministry it can, however, be of immediate value, just because it is possible to make a start on it at once, and time is quite definitely running out. It can help us to begin with the selection and training of men who will subsequently take on more than diaconal responsibilities.

In the last few years a very great deal has been written upon the question of priestly celibacy. There can be no doubt that this is a vital element in our present ministerial crisis, but it is only one of several. Raising the ban on the marriage of priests would certainly not solve by itself most of our old problems and it would undoubtedly at the same time create a number of new ones. There are in fact at least five highly practical inter-connected issues to be borne in mind with regard to the restructuring of the ordained ministry. They are as follows. Firstly, standards of education. There is absolutely no reason to think that there is one single standard of education inherently fitting to the priesthood; nor need we hold that in a particular age all priests should have about the same educational level. The functions of a priest are ministerial, correlative to a community, and his education should relate substantially to the type of ministry to which he is called, the work he is to do, the general educational level of the people whom he is going to serve. Too much education in some may be almost as much of an obstacle as too little in others. A long formal education may simply unfit a man for ministry in a remote area far from people of his own educational standard. It is clear that in the social situation of modern Africa it is of prime importance to have a good number of very well-educated priests, but it is almost equally clear that there is also a vital need for an even greater number of less highly qualified ones.

Secondly, finance. If the church in Eastern Africa had three times as many priests as at present, on the same terms, it would not be able to pay them. Indeed, it cannot pay its present numbers and with a steady decrease in availability of foreign mass stipends, the position is becoming steadily more serious. It is also probable that other large sources of foreign money—especially from Germany and America—may soon diminish. We need more priests, but we cannot well find the money to pay them. Here again the system needs to be changed. For one thing, financial support is related to the educational level of those to be supported. For another, and more fundamentally, there is the question whether the church need accept financial responsibility for all its ministers. The answer to that is clearly, in principle, 'No'. An almost essential part of the present ministerial system in much of Africa is the church's regular support of its local clergy with mass stipends and other funds deriving from another continent. In principle this system is a monstrosity, and if a restructuring of the financial aspects of ministry forces us to a restructuring of other aspects as well, that is only to be expected in a world where finance enters into the heart of things.

Thirdly, 'full-time' or 'part-time' priests. As a matter of

fact, no priest can spend all his time on strictly ministerial work, but all that he does should somehow share in the glow of his priesthood. Priests divide their time between five categories of occupation: (a) personal activities: eating, sleeping, recreation, private letter writing; (b) strictly priestly activity—celebrating mass, hearing confessions, anointing the sick; (c) apostolic activity of a kind fully proper also to the non-ordained—visiting the sick, marriage counselling, teaching religion in school; (d) ecclesiastical administration at parochial, diocesan or national level; this is not directly apostolic, but may be said to provide the necessary infra-structure for organised apostolic work; (e) other useful and gainful activities of one kind and another—farming, teaching history or mathematics, scholarship. Every priest includes in his life (a), (b) and (c); most include a measure of (d); some are predominantly concerned with (e). The point is that only (b) is formally priestly, and this occupies very few hours indeed in the lives of most priests. Some priests are today mostly occupied with (c) and/or (d), some with (e); of the latter some are church supported, some are supported by the secular work they do. There is no theological principle to indicate how the hours of the ordained should mostly be filled; to what extent general apostolic work should be done by the laity, to what extent by the clergy (as a matter of fact, in the best African dioceses the larger part is certainly already done by laity); what proportion of priests should spend the greater part of their working hours on (e).

In one situation it may be better to have in all few priests, occupied as much as possible with activities (c) and (d); in another situation it may be better that the lives of most priests very much include (e), and that (c) is carried out far more on a lay apostolate basis with merely a certain stiffening from the ordained on a full-time basis. This is in fact already the tendency in many countries today, including African countries. The question of church financial support for the ordained will depend very largely on the extent to which (e) is or is not included in their lives since this determines their capacity to maintain themselves.

Fourthly, the most suitable age for ordination is something we need to consider more carefully. It is not self-evident that the middle twenties is the ideal age. There is a strong tendency in many countries today towards mature entry; this again cannot but have a considerable effect upon the whole pattern of ministry and ministerial training.

Fifthly, the question of compulsory celibacy has to be raised within the context of the preceding issues. Certain answers to earlier questions have important implications for the celibacy question; equally, the insistence upon celibacy closes many options. Thus a celibate clergy must be a rather highly educated clergy, must normally be a clergy which is selected and ordained young, and it tends to be a clergy which is accustomed to practise community life. Within the total context there can be no doubt at all that maintenance of the rule of celibacy for all priests will prevent any serious restructuring of the ministry. Openness on this point is essential if we are to find a viable way forward.

The facts of the situation indicate quite clearly that our present system, seen as a whole, is undoubtedly leading the church to rapid disaster; necessary ministerial functions are simply not being performed at all, or are not being performed by those adequate to the task. Basically, our present pattern of ministry is not related effectively to our pattern of community. Change is called for, but change must be organic, relating to the total social situation and to the whole system of ministry, not just to a single element in one or the other. It is only through a sufficiently broad consideration of all the basic issues that we can develop a viable ministry.

The system we do develop must be capable of being varied to suit the situation. The copperbelt presents a very different problem from a sparsely populated and economically poor area such as Karema or Kigoma; a diocese which

has today no African priests cannot be treated in the same
way as one that has seventy. There must be a variety of detailed solutions. But I would suggest that everywhere there
are four elements which must enter substantially into the
new pattern of pastoral and missionary ministry. The first
is an active laity, taking its responsibilities in a largely collective way through pastoral and parish councils; a laity
which in one way or another will take over many of the
duties at present performed individually by priests and catechists. The second is a small, highly trained group of full-
time priests: those with roughly the present type of seminary training, only improved and reinforced. The duty of
this group cannot be to carry out the ordinary pastoral
work and celebration of the sacraments in the mass of
christian communities throughout the land, though they
will continue to do some of that; but their numbers are far
too small. Its work will be more one of pastoral over-sight,
episkopē in the broad sense; it will include regular visits to
all parishes, the giving of special courses of instruction to
many different groups of christians, the more prolonged
training of those participating in various other forms of
ministry, diocesan administration. The presence of such a
type of senior ordained ministry is, after all, one of the most
traditional things in the church.

The third group is a far larger body of priests, mostly
married, largely self-supporting, who will preside over the
eucharist in the great majority of local communities and
explain the word of God Sunday by Sunday. We already
have the core of this group among the more able catechists
and in fact their existence is about the most encouraging
thing the church in Africa at present has. But they are, on
the whole, not suitable for the urban areas. Here we must
look much more to natural leaders among both manual
workers and professional people. Some of this new group
of priests will, then, be upgraded catechists, some will be
townsmen of considerable secular education; some will have
another full-time occupation, others will be men already

retired from their main civil activities; all will be mature men of real prestige in their community with a proved christian life behind them plus special training before incorporation into the ordained ministry. We can take it for granted that in the Catholic Church of the future the majority of priests are likely to be married.

The fourth element is that of sisters. Almost everywhere we have far more sisters than we have priests. Hitherto they have worked in schools and hospitals, but have only entered rather slightly into general missionary and pastoral work. A wider use should now be made of them, as is indeed being done in some countries, notably Brazil. They can work in teams for catechetical instruction, pastoral visitation, refresher courses and 'missions' of all kinds, and I am sure they could bring a very valuable and enthusiastic stiffening to the work of the church. Such is the existing shortage of priests in Uganda that sisters have in fact already taken over the pastoral work in several parishes in the dioceses of Hoima and Fort Portal.

The problems of the ministry today cannot be solved in terms of any of these groups alone, or in terms of just two. Some people cry out for the lay apostolate, others for a great vocations campaign, others again for the ordination of catechists, or for the extensive handing over of the present functions of priests to nuns. None of these expedients alone will work effectively. A viable reform of the ministry depends, on the contrary, upon their solid integration, upon a rich, varied, flexible ministry to which God can and will call all sorts of people in many and diverse ways.

VI

It should be clear that the analysis we have made of the situation in much of Africa—for Tanzania, Uganda and Zambia are far from being unrepresentative of the rest—is in no way derived from a consideration of the problems or desires of other continents. It has been based on local facts and the new patterns of ministry proposed grow out of those facts and of no others. It would be an irresponsible calumny to say that in proposing such arguments one is simply trying to push on to Africa the desires of Europeans. Nothing could be further from the truth. I have no close experience of the ministerial situation in Europe and have myself given little thought to the particular ways the ministry there will need to be shaped, but I have much experience of the African situation, and also much concern.

Certainly, and quite naturally, in many things all parts of the universal church can and may tend in a common direction. I have no doubt that from some points of view this is true with regard to the ministry. Everywhere the tendency is towards a greater number of christians and a smaller number of professional 'full-time' ministers, but the speed of growth here in Africa, the absence of deeply rooted ecclesial institutions and the urgent stress in every side of life upon 'localisation', all this should force the church in Africa to adapt the shape of its ministry faster and more radically than is demanded elsewhere, the only alternative being large-scale ecclesial collapse. The church in Africa has in fact the great opportunity, as well as the need, vigorously to pioneer a new pattern of ministry combining marriage with ordination, to the great ultimate advantage of the whole church. The decision in June 1970 by the bishops of Gabon, Chad, the Central African Republic, Congo-Brazzaville and the Cameroons to ask the Pope for permission to ordain married men as the only possible way 'to answer the most elementary pastoral needs' is a welcome step forward on the road of realism. It is deplorable that others should see this, both untheologically and unhistorically, as lack of faith or, even more absurdly, as contempt for the African church.

A structural revolution in the whole pattern of the African church is required not merely because the present pattern of ministry is simply not viable, but because the whole mission of the church in the non-western world calls

for it. The factors which have prevented a deep accultura-
tion of the church in the past in Africa and Asia and which
still maintains today its heavily 'western' character throughout the world are, more than anything else, that the Catholic Church especially has been dominated by its clergy, and
that its clergy has been dominated by expatriates both
numerically and through the established patterns of training and living. Ministerial rigidity (going so far as recruiting nearly all future priests at about the age of twelve and
then subjecting them to thirteen years or more of segregated
institutional training) has been the source of the mental
and spiritual rigidity of the church as a whole which has
given it its strikingly western character in almost all parts
of the globe.

Moreover the present system can only be maintained if
there continues to be for decades a very large western labour
force doing much of the general work of the ministry in all
the churches of Africa. But the continuance of this labour
force—more than half of the total number of priests in each
country—would make it effectively impossible for the
church to mature as a truly local church, offering its own
contribution to the dialogue of the universal communion
and witnessing with strength and confidence within its own
local society. Without a renewal of the patterns of ministry
which will free these young local churches from this so
heavy dependence on the white western world their whole
possible effectiveness for mission and communion in the
world context will be imperilled.

Pastoral decline and evangelical ineffectiveness could be
the fruits of the present system even without a vast increase
in the size of the population. But this also is happening,
and the increase is very largely destined to be a christian
one. The Catholic Church in Africa today, though it is
already bursting at the seams, is small in comparison with
what it is bound to be in thirty years time.

In *Church and Mission in Modern Africa* (p. 212) I
offered the following prognosis:

	Catholics in Africa	Priests	Ratio
1966	27,000,000	15,000	1 : 1,800
1980	52,000,000	21,000	1 : 2,400
2000	112,000,000	32,000	1 : 3,500

I remarked on this that 'these forecasts are based on the most favourable assumptions: actually future ratios may well be far worse'. It is obvious to me now that unless the whole pattern of ministry is altered they will indeed be far, far worse. For one thing 112,000,000 is almost certainly a serious under-estimate. David Barrett has recently surveyed the field of future church growth and forecasts an African Catholic population in the year 2000 of 175,000,000 in a total christian population of 351,000,000.[10] The whole population of Africa at that time will be, according to United Nations estimates, 768 million. Barrett's forecast is based on a 1970 estimate of Catholic population (including catechumens) of 45 million. I suspect that this is an exaggeration and that the total for the year 2000 will also be less; but I don't think we will be going far wrong if we suggest a minimum for that year of 140 million.

Secondly, the estimate of 32,000 Catholic priests now seems an extremely unlikely one. I suggested that there could be 12,000 Africans and 20,000 missionaries. In 1970 there are less than 4,000 African priests and about 12,500 missionaries (excluding Morocco, Algeria, Tunisia, Libya and Egypt). As regards African secular priests we have had the following ordinations in the last ten years in the countries looked after by the Congregation of *Propaganda Fide*:[11]

[10] D. Barrett, 'A.D. 2000: 350 Million Christians in Africa' in *International Review of Missions*, January 1970, pp. 39–54. A few months earlier in the *Church Growth Bulletin*, May 1969, p. 74, he had suggested 167 million. It is, of course, impossible to make an exact forecast: there are too many unknown factors involved.

[11] These figures are taken from the annual editions of the *Status Seminariorum Indigenarum*; they include white South Africans.

1959	110
1960	111
1961	119
1962	157
1963	178
1964	158
1965	160
1966	181
1967	102
1968	135

This gives an average of 141 a year. Note that the Catholic population almost doubled in these ten years but there has been little increase in the already very meagre number of ordinations. Besides these there are a few others: there are, firstly, a few seculars from these territories not included in the *Propaganda* lists because they were ordained neither in Africa nor in Rome, but elsewhere in Europe or North America; but these will be very few. Secondly, there are those of Mozambique, Angola, Ethiopia and other small areas not subject to *Propaganda*. The total number of major seminarists in all these countries in 1969 was 197 (as against 2,388 in the countries subject to *Propaganda*). They will certainly not have an average of more than 15 ordinations a year. There are, thirdly, a small number of African religious priests. These are not very numerous, but there are Jesuits in the Congo, Oblates of Mary Immaculate in southern Africa, and a few others elsewhere. They might have twelve ordinations a year. Altogether, there will certainly not have been an average of more than 175 priests ordained a year in sub-Saharan Africa over the last ten years. To reach 12,000 by the year 2000, we will need at least an average of 250 ordinations in this decade, 300 after 1980, and 400 after 1990. That is not impossible but it is also very far from assured as things are going at present.

As regards the number of missionaries, it was little short of absurd to suggest that they could rise in these thirty

years from 12,500 to 20,000. Recruitment in almost all mission societies has fallen steadily and decisively in the last
few years and it is difficult to see the trend altering again,
at least for a considerable period. The average age of missionaries is also rather advanced. Hence, even if African
governments continue to admit foreign missionaries freely
over the next thirty years (and that is a very big if), a considerable decrease in the number of foreign priests working
in Africa is absolutely certain. It is, I think, fairly opti-
mistic to think that by the year 2000 there will be as many
as 8,000 still there. If we take that as a maximum, we could
arrive at a rough estimate of 12,000 Africans and 8,000
expatriates.

We would then arrive at the following prognosis:

	Catholics in Africa	Priests	Ratio
AD 2000	140,000,000	20,000	1 : 7,000

It could, of course, be still a good deal worse than this but
a ratio of 1 : 7,000 is certainly a far more realistic one than
1 : 3,500. It does, of course, mean a state of very large-scale
collapse, considerably worse than the present situation in
South America. Those in authority, whether in Rome or in
Africa, who today would continue to refuse to alter the pattern of priestly ministry are taking upon themselves responsibility for the most enormous ecclesial breakdown that
will ever have been witnessed in one short period of church
history—a breakdown due not to heresy, not to lack of faith
and zeal, but simply to a rigid adherence to unworkable
church structures in the very teeth of the evidence.

The whole future of the christian church as a credible
sacrament of divine love and human unity at world level
will depend in the coming generation upon escaping from
the historic identification of christianity and the white race.
The church in Africa and its vast growth in the last fifty
years does offer the possibility of just this, but the whole
thing can be brought almost to nought if decisions are not

taken, and taken soon, which will enable the Catholic Church in these countries to escape from its present overwhelming dependence in personnel and money upon the white countries, and to stand firmly upon its own feet. This is absolutely impossible without a reshaping of the ministry. The present pattern will make not only for an intolerable pastoral situation and the drying up of the evangelisation of the millions of non-christians but also for cultural sterility and a western ecclesial hang-over in societies which in other fields have long managed to dispense with such massive outside support and control.

10

FROM MISSION TO CHURCH IN BUGANDA

I

There are in history particular moments which achieve a
classical quality of memorableness. In the lengthy history of
British government the events of the Long Parliament in
1639 to 1641 stand out in such a way. There was an exhilara-
tion, a sense of breakthrough which the rough and tumble
of subsequent years, disillusionment, a return to conditions
of accepted mediocrity have never effaced.

In the vast and complex story of missionary work in
modern Africa, the first years of the church in Buganda[1]
attained a quality of these dimensions. Doubtless the entire
setting of the state of Buganda and the court of Mutesa,

[1] Buganda now forms the central region of the Republic of Uganda.
It was an ancient kingdom ruled by its hereditary monarch or *Kabaka*.
(The people of Buganda are called *Baganda* [singular: *Muganda*], but
the root Ganda is used alone more and more as a qualifying adjective.)
It became a British Protectorate in the 1890s, but the Protectorate was
gradually enlarged by the British occupation of adjacent territories
until Buganda became but one—though a privileged—part of a new
political entity, Uganda. The relationship between these two became
increasingly tense as the privileged status inevitably diminished until
the monarchy together with Buganda's separate parliament (the
Lukiko) were abolished in 1966. Ecclesiastically, both for Catholics and
Protestants, Buganda is today divided into two dioceses, of Kampala
and Masaka, the former being for Catholics an archdiocese. Finally, it
may be noted that by 'Protestant' Anglican is meant throughout; in
Uganda Anglicans have been and are today normally described as
Protestants. This chapter is offered as an ecumenical case study of the
growth of the church in a highly influential but far from typical area.

already depicted in such glowing terms by Henry Stanley, have contributed to this effect. The character of the leading missionaries, Mackay and Lourdel, had their part to play. Still more important was the dynamic quality of the young christians involved: Mukasa, Lwanga, Kalemba the Mulumba, Andrew Kaggwa and others. The martyrdoms, the strange subsequent history of exile and civil war, the final settlement and the quite exceptional growth of the church in the following years: all these factors contributed to make of the years in Buganda after 1877 an epic in which the men involved, the twists of events, the rise and fall of fortune, remain imprinted on the mind with a clarity which time does not dim and which history affords to few of its subjects.

Clearly we are indebted for our awareness of these years, not only to the writings of many of those involved, missionary and non-missionary, and the genuine oral traditions which still survive, but also to subsequent writers who have studied what happened in a way that is perhaps unique for nineteenth century African history: Sir Apolo Kagwa, Sir John Gray, Fathers Thoonen and Faupel, Miss Margery Perham, Canon Taylor, Professor Low, to mention only some of those whose research and published work have thrown light on these vital, tumultuous years in which the church in Uganda was born.[2]

2 Among the more recent literature Father Faupel's *African Holocaust* (Chapman, 1965) takes pride of place for the study of the first christian decade. It is, of course, a revision of Fr Thoonen's *Black Martyrs*. More recently Louise Pirouet has written a brief but very clear account of the martyrs entitled *Strong in Faith*, 1969. Canon John Taylor's *Growth of the Church in Buganda* (SCM Press, 1958) is a work of major importance and the present study owes very much to it. Of other general works Roland Oliver's *Missionary Factor in East Africa* (1952; second edition with a new introduction, 1965) is still worth consulting; there are also E. Matheson's *An Enterprise so Perilous* (Mellifont), a study of nineteenth century White Father work in East Africa, and H. P. Gale's *Uganda and the Mill Hill Fathers* (Macmillan, 1959) which goes up to 1914. It is a pity that the last work is orientated in so exclusively missionary a way.

For the nineteenth century three specialised studies are of particular value: D. A. Low, *Religion and Society in Buganda 1875-1900*, East

II

It is obvious that a new church will normally begin from
a 'mission' and with missionaries, but the theological relationship between mission and church, whose actual working
out in the particular context of Uganda I wish to examine,
is itself a complex one.[3]

'Church' refers to the totality of the christian fellowship,
both local and universal, 'mission' to its service and outgoing action. But as the church can have ultimate meaning
only in terms of its function, of the striving after that purpose for which Christ launched it, it can be said that it is
only in terms of its mission that the church herself can be
interpreted. Mission is not an occasional event in the life of
the community like a sudden swarm of bees from the hive,
after which everyone can settle down again to an internally
directed existence, it has instead to be a constant movement,
the most decisive permanent dimension of christian living

African Studies, a seminal essay; the same author's *Converts and
Martyrs in Buganda* (pages 150–163 of *Christianity in Tropical Africa*,
edited C. G. Baeta, Oxford, 1968), useful especially for its evaluation
of Mutesa's later years; J. A. Rowe, *The Purge of Christians at
Mwanga's Court*, Journal of African History, vol. V, 1964, 1, pp. 55–72.
This last is an excellent study of the years 1885–6. Margery Perham's
Lugard, the Years of Adventure, 1858–1898 (Collins, 1956), and the
massively detailed three volumes of the *Diaries of Lord Lugard*, edited
M. Perham (Faber & Faber, 1959) help greatly for the years 1890–2,
but these need to be balanced by J. A. Rowe, *Lugard at Kampala*,
Makerere History Paper, 1969. What the history of Buganda at present
lacks is a full study of the crucial developments in 1887–9, although
Sir John Gray's article 'The Year of the Three Kings of Buganda
1888–1889', *Uganda Journal*, 1950, pp. 15–52, provides a most valuable
basis for this. There is also far too little generally available on White
Father work after 1892.

[3] It is impossible to refer here adequately to the vast modern theological literature on the church-mission relationship, but reference may
be made to C. Couturier, *The Mission of the Church* (Helicon Press:
Darton, Longman & Todd), 1960, first published in French, 1957;
H.-W. Gensichen, *Living Mission* (Fortress Press, Philadelphia, 1966):
much in John Taylor's book listed above, and the first chapters of my
own *Church and Mission in Modern Africa* (Burns & Oates, 1967).

both at the level of world church and at that of a healthy local church. It exactly balances the other dimension of union, coming together, communion. Mission, then, cannot be understood simply in a geographical sense and the establishment of new local churches; it is to be carried on in many ways and circumstances where that is not called for. In its absence any church becomes 'churchy' and inward-turned. Nevertheless the mission to the wholly beyond and the consequent planting of a new local church ('missionary activity' in the more traditional sense) remains its apex and most striking expression, and it is that aspect of mission with which we are chiefly concerned here.

Examining christian life in Uganda we will label it as 'mission' in so far as it is still dependent upon overseas christian bodies in a way that a full local church is not, while we label it as 'church' in so far as it has become a self-ministering, self-supporting, self-propagating body—a rounded local fellowship of christians in faith, sacrament and service, a self-reliant community, itself obedient to the call of mission.

Nevertheless we have here to remember that a local christian church cannot be by the nature of the case a wholly independent entity. There are churches throughout the world, but there is and has still to be the one church. It is evidently the missionary task to establish a new local church in such a way that it is a living part of the world communion. And a living part means a giving and taking part. It is natural moreover that old well-established churches should continue in a special way to help young ones. It is not easy to say apodictically how much continuing help is proper within a healthy communion between two such churches and how much indicates rather an unhealthy mission domination over new christians, but it is clear that the latter has too often happened. Missions have continued for centuries, never becoming truly churches, but remaining dependent generation after generation on a ministry, both episcopal and presbyteral, coming from abroad. It has to be admitted that this has been a fault particularly characteristic of post-Reformation Catholic missionary work.

III

These general observations may help us in our judgment on the course of growth in the two churches established in Uganda, the Roman Catholic and the Church of Uganda.[4] Their origins date from almost exactly the same time. The Anglican missionaries, the Reverend C. T. Wilson and Lieutenant Shergold-Smith, arrived in June 1877 but the latter was murdered south of the lake a few months later; Wilson withdrew twice in the next months and the CMS mission was only really established on Wilson's return with Alexander Mackay in November 1878. Three months later, February 17, 1879, Père Lourdel and Brother Amans landed at Entebbe.

At that time Mackay was twenty-nine years old and Lourdel twenty-five. They were to be the two dominant figures of the early years. Both were men of great faith, highly intelligent, daring, energetic, rather hasty. Mackay excelled in his practical capacity as a craftsman and engineer. Lourdel in his tact, charm of character and ability as a counsellor. Both died early in 1890 just before the frequently tragic and finally decisive events of 1891–2 which, under the direction of Lugard, established a radically new milieu for the churches to live and work within.[5] The British Raj had begun.

Within a few months of the passing of the two great

4 The church of Uganda, Rwanda and Burundi is a province of the Anglican communion. A joint study of the two communions in Uganda whose history is in many ways so similar is not made easier by the quite extraordinary hostility each felt for the other through many years. Missionary literature on each side abounds in the most sweeping condemnations of the other. Happily this is now passing. The present study completely ignores this aspect of missionary work and church growth, but it cannot be denied that it was often almost uppermost in the minds of the founding fathers of the church in Uganda.

5 Alexander Mackay left Buganda in 1887 and did not return. He

pioneers, the two outstanding figures of the church of the next generation had arrived, their arrival indeed curiously mirroring that of the earlier pair just twelve years earlier. Bishop Tucker entered Uganda on December 27 1890, Father Streicher on February 21 1891.[6] It is in fact strange how completely December 1890 marks a new beginning as regards the European presence in Buganda. Mgr Hirth, replacing Livinhac, arrived for the first time on December 8. Captain Lugard reached Kampala ten days later, the 18th. Bishop Tucker got in after another nine days, December 27. Such a spate of arrivals must have greatly helped to build up Ganda tensions. It is worth remembering too that the only

---

died south of the lake at Usambiro in February 1890. Siméon Lourdel died at Rubaga on May 12 1890. He was in fact the first European to die in Buganda, but Bishop Hannington had, of course, been murdered nearly five years earlier (October 29 1885) inside what is modern Uganda.

It is not easy to state the exact relative importance of Fathers Lourdel and Livinhac in the early White Father mission. Father Lourdel receives the central place in all narratives. Fr Livinhac was the first local superior of the Buganda mission and was certainly the one responsible for major decisions. And it was he who composed the first Luganda grammar. However he was in Buganda a far shorter time than Lourdel. The latter opened the mission in February 1879 and was joined by Livinhac in June. They were both there until the general departure in November 1882. After the return, however, Livinhac was present for only brief periods; he was by now bishop and responsible also for the missions south of the lake and Lourdel had taken over as local superior of the Buganda mission. Livinhac visited Buganda briefly May–June 1886 at the height of the persecution; he was back there in 1888 and shared in the general October expulsion; he next returned in March and April 1890 before leaving for Algiers to become Vicar General of the Society, Lourdel dying one month after his departure.

6 Bishop Tucker was born in 1849. He retired from Uganda in 1911 and died in England June 15 1914. Tucker's two volumed work *Eighteen Years in Uganda and East Africa* (Edward Arnold, 1908) contains much information on the early years.

Bishop Streicher was born in 1863; he retired from his vicariate in 1933 but remained in Uganda. He died at Villa Maria, the mission he had founded sixty years earlier, June 7 1952 and is buried there. Reference can be made to Sir John Gray's warm tribute to him in the *Uganda Journal*, 1953, pp. 63–67, and to the lengthy work of J. Cussac, *Evêque et Pionnier, Monseigneur Streicher* (Paris, 1955).

remaining White Father with real experience, P. Denoit, died a few months later, in May 1891.[7]

December 1890 marked indeed a new beginning both for church and state. Tucker and Streicher were the two men destined to have a decisive influence on the growth of their two communions in the next quarter century and it was largely due to them personally that both missions continued quite emphatically as churches in a way that has not happened nearly so clearly in many other parts of Africa.

IV

One cannot help but be impressed by the almost staggeringly self-assured approach of the first christian converts to their new religious life. The Baganda, members of a society in some ways surprisingly free and self-confident, seem to have been looking at that time for a religion and a possibility of personal commitment superior to that of their traditional gods. There had been a very real interest in islam in the preceding years and some had died for it. Now the story was to be repeated.[8] Certainly this sense of a real quest for religion is not something missionaries encountered in many parts of Africa; here too, special circumstances helped to turn it early into a truly mature christian commitment.

The local church began quickly. The White Fathers baptised four converts on March 27 1880 and four more on

[7] Several of the most able Catholic missionaries of the next generation—Guillermain, Achte and Marcou among others—arrived the same day as Streicher, February 21. The speed with which the journey from Europe could now be made is shown by the fact that they brought with them *The Times* up to October 3, and sent them to Lugard the next day! See *Diaries*, II, p. 96.

Guillermain succeeded Hirth as bishop north of the lake in 1895 but died almost at once (July 14 1896). He is buried at Bukalasa.

The very remarkable Anglican missionaries of the coming years—men like Baskerville, Pilkington the Bible translator and Roscoe the anthropologist—arrived either with Tucker or shortly after.

[8] This is a point Low well makes in his *Converts and Martyrs in Buganda*.

May 14. However from then on they were tied by Cardinal Lavigerie's instructions, received June 1 1880, enjoining a four year catechumenate. After further correspondence and a strong protest from Livinhac, some exceptions were after all to be allowed and they baptised eight more two years later, April–May 1882, among them Joseph Mukasa, Andrew Kaggwa and Matthias Kalemba. They were all carefully picked men and they formed the nucleus of the Catholic Church.[9]

The Anglican missionaries made their first baptism the same year, 1882, while in 1883 the number they baptised was quite considerable. Yet despite this and the continued presence of the Anglican missionaries all through the next critical years, one has the impression that it was the Catholics who were growing stronger and who provided by far the greater part of the leadership in the months of persecution, 1885–6.

I cannot help believing that the decisive reason for this, paradoxically enough, was precisely the sudden departure of the White Fathers from the country in November 1882 for reasons which have never been properly explained.[10]

[9] Cardinal Lavigerie's extremely rigid instructions of 1879 allowing no baptisms, except in case of the dying, without a four year catechumenate are to be found in *Instructions aux Missionnaires* (Editions Grands Lacs, 1950), pp. 109–110. They were repeated in a letter to Livinhac, dated from Algiers October 18 1880. At this date he had presumably heard of the baptisms of that year, but did not know that Livinhac had now received his 1879 instructions. He therefore appended a further copy and added: 'Mes prescriptions sont des ordres exprès, que je vous donne de concert avec le Saint-Siège Apostolique; elles vous obligent donc en conscience' (*Instructions*, p. 143). Livinhac had already written back a strong protest against these instructions which is reflected in Lavigerie's letter of February 10 1881: 'Cela me conduit à vous parler des règles que je vous ai données pour le catéchuménat et contre lesquelles vous me paraissez réclamer avec une vivacité que je ne comprends pas' (p. 168). However he agreed to permit exceptions for those willing to die for their faith! As a result of this permission the eight baptisms of 1882 were able to take place with quite incalculable consequences for the young church.

[10] In a letter of Cardinal Lavigerie, dated March 24 1883, he still

6

They only returned in July 1885, two years and eight
months later. It is worth recording that Joseph Mukasa
Balikudembe was martyred only four months after their return, in November. It is strange how much Father Lourdel
has been given the centre of the picture in the years preceding the martyrdoms because it is clear from a careful
study of the evidence that it was in his absence rather than
his presence that the church became really strong. The
Catholics now had to stand entirely on their own feet. Their
chief leaders, Mukasa and Kalemba, had only been baptised
six months before the missionaries departed. Here was the
church: sixteen men, most of them fairly young, recently
baptised, and a considerably larger group of catechumens.
One might certainly have expected that in the coming years
they would have merged with the Protestants—Mackay did
not leave the country—or just faded away. In fact just the
opposite happened. They grew into a genuine self-reliant,
self-propagating church and it was surely those years of full
responsibility and leadership that prepared so many for
future martyrdom.

It is a fascinating picture, something nearer to New
Testament christian life than has almost ever occurred.
There were in fact a group of 'house churches'. There was,
first of all, the church in the King's court led by Joseph
Mukasa. Secondly, there was the church in and around the
house of Matthew Kisule, the gunsmith, at Natete; thirdly,
a group in the household of the young chief Alexis Sebbowa.
Fourthly, there was the community fifty miles away at
Mityana built up by Kalemba. It is thought that by the time
of the martyrdoms there were some two hundred believing
christians at Mityana, a place where no missionary had ever

clearly knew nothing of the departure from Uganda of the previous
November. Indeed he speaks instead of the probable departure of the
CMS missionaries (*Instructions*, pp. 200–201). But he had heard about it
by August. Two years later, in a letter to Livinhac of August 1885, he
speaks of the return to Uganda, 'cette mission si malheureusement
interrompue par de vaines terreurs' (p. 216).

come. Certainly many of these christians had not seen a priest even once. Lourdel estimated on his return in 1885 that the total count of Catholics, baptised and catechumens, was now upwards of eight hundred. If the freedom of outlook and missionary method of New Testament times had been retained, some of these apostles would surely have been ordained priests; instead of that the missionaries could still hesitate as to the propriety of even baptising some of the firmest believers! It seems to have been Joseph Mukasa's martyrdom which really convinced Lourdel on this point, and it is moving to remember that the new leader—Lwanga —was baptised the very day (November 15) the old one died. Yet there was still over-much hesitation. Lourdel in his diary gives the impression of feeling he must justify himself for this action.[11] At one moment it was actually Charles Lwanga who had to take the matter into his own hands and baptise four of his companions on the very eve of martyrdom. Lwanga, like Mukasa, was after all no younger than Lourdel himself had been when he arrived in Buganda, while many of the others were far older.[12] One feels already a strain between missionary preconceptions and methods and the real needs and possibilities of the young church.

If I have here concentrated upon the Catholics in these years, it is just because—for partly accidental reasons as I have suggested—they seem to have become a more vigorous community, a more genuine church. Mackay once sensed part of the trouble when he wrote regretfully: 'There is so much in our ways and methods that strengthens the idea of foreign rule . . . English men, English church, English

---

[11] 'How could we refuse them this grace?': Faupel, *African Holocaust*, p. 119.

[12] There is still a tendency to talk of the converts rather indiscriminately as 'boys'. Thus Faupel calls Sebwato a 'boy', p. 116, when he must in fact have been in his middle forties! As Faupel himself remarks, Europeans often underestimate the age of Africans, and Lourdel himself seems to have done so with Lwanga (Faupel, p. 62). Only a minority of the martyrs, and none of their leaders, could possibly be described as boys.

formularies, English bishop'.[13] Perhaps as a Scot he was particularly sensitive to this! I suspect too that his own character
and his very skills as a craftsman more than a teacher had
something to do with it. But probably the very continuance
of his presence was the most decisive factor!

Mackay left Uganda for south of the lake in 1887, and
was followed by the remaining Anglican missionaries in the
general expulsion of the following year. It seems probable
that the very much more active role that the Baganda Protestants exercised in the coming years is again not uncon-
nected with that fact. With his departure Sebwato and
Kagwa took over the Protestant leadership, just as Mukasa
and Kalemba had done for the Catholics five years earlier.
However it was Honorat Nnyonintono, the new Catholic
leader, who held the christians as a whole together with remarkable statesmanship through the long crisis of 1888—
probably the gravest moment for the young church in the
whole story. His death in battle the next year was a major
tragedy. He was replaced as christian *katikiro* by Apolo
Kagwa, certainly another great statesman though he lacked
Honorat's capacity to hold the two christian groups together.

Upon both sides the experience of the 1880s, when for one
reason and another the young christians had had to stand in
crisis after crisis upon their own legs, make their own decisions, die their own deaths, and finally triumph in arms
when Gabriel Kintu recaptured the capital and restored
Mwanga to his throne in February 1890, it was that experience which was to be decisive for the future of the
young church. Only a relatively small group was, after all,
martyred.[14] The colleagues of Mukasa and Lwanga had remained to fight it out and then to provide a permanent core
of mature African lay leadership which had a profound
effect upon the development of church life in the next thirty

13 Quoted in Taylor, op. cit., p. 44. Mackay wrote this in 1877. It
was, of course, *mutatis mutandis*, true of all missions.
14 See the very clear treatment of this point by Rowe, op. cit.

years.[15] On the Catholic side men like Alexis Sebbowa and Stanislaus Mugwanya, on the Protestant side Nikodemo Sebwato, Ham Mukasa and Apolo Kagwa had all been christians through the time of persecution. The mantle of the fallen leaders had passed to them and it remained very markedly with some of them—Alexis and Stanislaus, Ham Mukasa and Apolo Kagwa—right into the 1930s and even after. Ham Mukasa, already a believer before the persecution, baptised in 1887, remained for decades a pillar of the Anglican Church. He became county chief of Kyagwe in 1905 and only died in 1956.[16]

It was such men clearly born to authority, conscious from the start of their responsibility for the church as for the state, who ensured that in the coming years of missionary preponderance the inheritance of the first age was not lost.

V

They were helped in this, as has already been suggested, by the two remarkable new missionary leaders who arrived in the country at the end of 1890. It is certain that the outlook of these two was at times strikingly different from that of

15 Of course, a further considerable number of these men died fighting in the six years following the martyrdoms. Thus, of the seven men who gave evidence before the White Fathers in 1887 on the subject of the martyrdoms—so providing the start for the canonisation process—three died in battle in the following years: Louis Kigongo, killed at Mengo in October 1888 when the Muslims drove the Christians out during Kiwewa's short reign; Charles Werabe, one of the three young men spared at Namugongo June 3 1886, fell at the same time as Nnyonintono in one of the battles of 1889; while Francis Kintu was killed fighting the Protestants at Mengo, January 24 1892 (Nicq, *Le père Siméon Lourdel*, p. 535, ³1922). The same day as Kintu, Sembera Mackay, one of the first five Protestants to be baptised (March 18 1882) died fighting on the other side. He had also been one of the first six 'lay evangelists' commissioned by Bishop Tucker just a year earlier. Lugard mentions him in his account of the fight (*Diaries* III, p. 32): 'Poor Sembera (the best fellow in Uganda, and the peacemaker) was shot by these first few shots and killed.'

16 There is a brief but pleasant memoir of Ham Mukasa in the *Uganda Journal* 1959, pp. 184–186.

many of their European fellow-workers. Of the two Tucker had, of course, the direction of his church from the start, while Streicher arrived as a junior missionary, and in March 1891 after only three weeks in the country was sent off westward to found a first mission in Buddu county, the heart of the later Masaka district.[17] Only six years later was he chosen bishop, travelled to Bukumbi south of the lake for consecration (August 15 1897), and then returned to exercise a decisive influence upon the Catholic Church for over thirty years.[18]

These years after 1890 were ones of constant missionary expansion and of a vast increase in the number of christians. By 1904 there were 79 CMS missionaries in the country, 83 members of the White Fathers society and 35 of the Mill Hill Fathers. Mission stations were being opened not only throughout Buganda but far away to the West and East. There is no doubt of the continued fervour and energy of the new converts. Nevertheless, the more the missionaries increased, the less room there seemed to be for African initiative—at least unless it could be channelled into a clear institutional pattern. Already in November 1892 the Anglican Baskerville could write: 'Our meeting with the elders on Saturday did a lot of good, and I think they will not be so independent in future.'[19] This almost inevitable attitude was characteristic of both churches, but perhaps particularly of the Catholics, and this just because the church institutions they took for granted were both more rigid and left less room for lay initiative than those of the Anglicans. Conditions required for ordination to the priesthood could not be

[17] Streicher had already learnt a good deal of the Luganda language before arrival with the aid of Livinhac's grammar. The next month, April, Mgr Hirth sent Achte and Marcou eastwards to begin work in Kyagwe, that being then the county ruled by Alexis Sebbowa (cf. G. Leblond, *Le Père Auguste Achte*, Maison Carrée, 1912, p. 137).

[18] He learnt of his appointment as bishop May 6 1897; he had, however, been ruling the vicariate as Provicar since the death of Mgr Guillermain the previous July.

[19] Quoted by Taylor, op. cit., p. 71.

modified; moreover there was no suggestion of the introduction of church councils with full lay participation: the latter were only to be introduced by Bishop Kiwanuka fifty years later. But in both communions the element of 'mission' increases, that of 'church' decreases.

However this was far from absolute. Both the strength and confidence of the African christians themselves and the clear aims of Tucker and Streicher, each operating according to the characteristic outlook of his church, prevented it.

Let us consider the pattern of Anglican growth first. A church council under the leadership of Sebwato was established as early as 1885 and some sharing of the laity in church government was an established reality from then on. Again, it is remarkable how much of pre-baptismal instruction in the early years was managed by the converts themselves—one passing on his knowledge to others with an enormous enthusiasm, husbands teaching their wives to read, and so on. But the most characteristic and striking feature of all in the church life of the 1890s was, perhaps, the catechist movement, the entry of Africans with a very great elan into a regular church ministry both at home and abroad. Already in 1891 Nathaniel Mudeka, a nephew of the old pagan Katikiro Mukasa, offered to work outside his own country and became a catechist south of the lake. In the next years Anglican Baganda catechists were going forth West, East, and North, evangelising new lands—Ankole, Toro, Bunyoro, and other places still further away. By 1906 six of them had reached as far as the famed Gondokoro in the Sudan.

It is right to recall here that this early Baganda missionary movement was—like so many other missionary movements in history—linked with a nationalist, even semi-imperialist, expansion. On the same roads tramped by catechists went other Baganda—chiefs and soldiers—and the Baganda catechist missionaries could suffer at times from the characteristic attitudes and limitations of an imperialist viewpoint. Crabtree, an early Anglican missionary visiting Bukedi early in 1901, had this to say: 'Amongst the Bakedi the language difficulty comes in: those boys or lads who join the Baganda and live with them and learn their language, are being taught slowly as at Bululu and Kikabukabu in the Lumo-gera district. Three years, and yet not a Muganda able to teach in the vernacular . . .'[20] Elsewhere, however, Crabtree did note a few exceptions to this, and the linguistic exertions of a man like Kivebulaya are well-known.

For Bishop Tucker the grade of catechist was the first rung in a continuous ladder of ecclesiastical ministry; from it the more reliable could rise higher. In 1893 he ordained his first deacons and three years later, May 31 1896, the first Baganda priests. This extremely rapid start with a local ministry, once a bishop was in the country, is surely remark-able. Of the early Anglican deacons some were great chiefs like Sebwato, but most of them were full time evangelists. Thus Mudeka was ordained a deacon in 1896 and priest three years later. In this way an African ministry with great devotion but naturally also a rather limited education was able to get under way with considerable rapidity.

The finest figure of all in this early Anglican ministry is surely that of Apolo Kivebulaya. Baptised in 1895, he volun-teered for the ministry two years later and was soon engaged both in studying at Namirembe and preaching the gospel in

[20] Quoted in John Gray, 'Kakunguru in Bukedi', *Uganda Journal*, 27, I, 1963, p. 41. For the general Ganda expansionism of this time see, among others, A. D. Roberts, *The Sub-Imperialism of the Baganda*, Journal of African History, III, 1962, 2, pp. 435–450. The tendency for some catechists to mix up evangelism and government can be illus-trated, for instance, by the Mill Hill Father Van Term's complaint to the authorities, dated October 4 1901, that in the eastern districts Baganda catechists settled down in the chief's compound and domi-nated civil proceedings (see Gale, *Uganda and the Mill Hill Fathers*, pp. 224–225). But it is hard to blame catechists for mixing up the two when so many missionaries had consistently done the same! The Baganda were not unique in sharing in the missionary expansion to neighbouring territories. Batoro and Banyoro did the same. For the whole subject see Louise Pirouet, *Evangelists and Subimperialists*, Dini na Mila, October 1969, pp. 28–41.

neighbouring villages. In a few months he was sent off to Toro. Ordained a deacon in 1900 and a priest in 1903, he had a long, holy, and arduous life of evangelisation in the Congo, dying in 1933 at Mboga where he had been a minister for thirty years.[21]

All this was magnificent, but it must be noted too that there were strict limits in the initiative allowed. The missionaries remained only too clearly in ultimate control. There was certainly no real parity of dignity between priests white and black. Bishop Tucker had earnestly striven for this, and his plans for a church constitution, first proposed as early as 1897, were extremely far-sighted and in the line of Henry Venn and the CMS tradition at its very best. They were, however, only accepted in a modified form in 1909, leaving the mission clearly above the local church. In the words of one of the earliest missionaries, Baskerville, a man—be it noted—who lived very close to the people indeed: 'To me the greatest objection seems to be the proposed equality of European and native workers, thereby in some cases placing Europeans under native control'.[22] With such an outlook a really self-confident local church could hardly be expected to develop. If a European handed over a job, it must always be so as to retire upwards. And as there were by now a good many Europeans about, this very effectively limited for many years a full development in the recognition of responsibility in the local church. It must be noted also that, despite Tucker's flexible approach to the ministry, the numbers ordained did in fact remain comparatively small: by 1914 there were no more than 33 native priests. It is striking too that though the first Anglican priests were ordained seventeen years before the first Catholic priests, the first Ugandan bishop was to be a Catholic.[23]

[21] Anne Luck, *African Saint*, the story of Apolo Kivebulaya, London (SCM Press), 1963.

[22] Quoted by Taylor, op. cit., p. 87.

[23] The first African to be consecrated a bishop in the Church of Uganda was Bishop Balya from Toro; he was consecrated in 1947 as an

Turning to the Catholic effort in these years, we see some things very similar, others rather different. The enormous initial enthusiasm, the vast catechism classes of the 90s and their self-help system were the same; so too was the catechist movement. When Streicher took over the vicariate in 1897 there were already, apparently, 243 recognised catechists and they were soon penetrating as far afield as their Protestant counterparts.[24] A group of Catholic Baganda catechists was settled in Teso by 1903. The saintly Yohana Kitagana, baptised in 1896, had set out for Bunyoro in 1901 and he continued his work with utter devotion in the western region for nearly forty years, dying in Kigezi in July 1939. It is worth noting that both the Anglican Kivebulaya and the Catholic Kitagana worked as celibates, a condition obligatory neither for the Anglican priest nor for the Catholic catechist, but freely embraced by both as helpful to evangelism.

Bishop Streicher was as anxious as Bishop Tucker to have African priests, but there was for him no possibility of promoting a catechist in this direction. He would perhaps have been willing to do so for Cardinal Lavigerie had himself written to Pope Leo XIII on July 1 1890 proposing a married priesthood for Africa.[25] This was however rejected

auxiliary for western Uganda. He has now retired but is still alive and active.

24 There was at first no regular training school. The beginnings of one date from the end of 1902, see a letter from Father Matthews to Bishop Hanlon mentioning the project: Gale, op. cit., p. 239. Initially at Rubaga, the following year it was already installed at Mitala Maria. Bishop Streicher used to visit it annually and make an appeal for volunteers to work outside Buganda (*Notices nécrologiques*, Société des Missionnaires d'Afrique, 1952, pp. 3–47). Later on the school was again moved to Bikira, south of Masaka.

25 'La question qui se pose sérieusement à l'esprit, c'est s'il ne conviendrait pas d'accorder le mariage des prêtres indigènes à tous les noirs d'Afrique. . . . C'est là, sans doute, un grave problème; mais il ne suffit pas d'en voir les difficultés, il faut le décider un jour et je crois qu'il serait digne de votre sainteté après tout ce qu'elle a déjà daigné de faire pour les noirs de faire prendre l'initiative d'une telle étude par la S. Congrégation de la Propagande.'

by the Holy Office. The road to the priesthood was to be a different one. The Catholic Church was not prepared to accept a basically different or lower standard for its black priests than for its white. The extensive knowledge of Latin required together with the obligation of celibacy raised great difficulties. But the early White Fathers were not to be deterred. It was in fact Mgr Hirth who began the work as early—almost unbelievably—as 1893, in which year Fr Marcou was put in charge of a group of boys stationed at Villa Maria, Fr Streicher's own mission. Even Streicher had at first been doubtful as to the wisdom of starting such a thing so quickly. It was the explicit instruction of the Cardinal Prefect of Propaganda that convinced him: 'A mission that can produce martyrs can produce priests'.[26] From that moment Streicher put all his weight behind this work and drove his often reluctant missionaries on: 'This is the chief work of my vicariate'.

The seminary was at first somewhat peripatetic. It moved from Villa to Rubaga, and Rubaga to Kisubi, only returning to the Villa Maria parish and settling down at Bukalasa in 1903, when Fr Marcou ceased to be superior. At the same moment the 'major seminary' became an independent entity, going to Bikira. They were however reunited at Bukalasa two years later, the senior institution being finally established on its own at Katigondo only in 1911.[27]

Nothing is more impressive than the immense and

[26] Quoted in the *Notice nécrologique* of Mgr Streicher, p. 22. The unquestioning acceptance of these instructions in face of apparently insuperable obstacles is a good example of the way the very Ultramontane formation of the White Fathers stood them in good stead.

[27] *Registre du personnel du Petit Séminaire de la Sainte Famille, Bukalasa*. When the major seminary was brought to Bukalasa from Bikira in 1905 there were in all eight major seminarians, of these three became priests: Bazilio Lumu, Victor Mukasa (both ordained June 29 1913) and Yoanna Muswabuzi (ordained March 7 1915). Fr Lumu died in March 1946, Fr Muswabuzi on Christmas Day 1967. Both are buried at Bukalasa. Mgr Victor Mukasa is still alive and active at the time of writing.

persistent effort involved in this project and the refusal to abandon it in spite of the apparently overwhelming difficulties.[28] Among them the production of textbooks in Luganda for a suitable minor seminary course of ecclesiastical and humanistic studies was itself a herculean task in those early years, above all the writing and then printing of a full Luganda-Latin dictionary and grammar. I must confess to finding the dry 632 pages of the *Lexikon Latinum Ugandicum*, printed at Bukalasa in 1912 but in manuscript use much earlier, an intensely moving document.[29] Certainly in men like Fathers Gorju and Le Veux, Streicher had linguists fully adequate for tasks such as these.[30]

It is safe to claim that at least between the years 1903 and 1922 there was no other institution in the whole of Uganda which offered an education of comparable academic level to

[28] It is not unfair to make the comparison with the seminary at Bagamoyo, begun at the first mission on the East African coast, in the late 1860s, but allowed to die a natural death in face of great difficulties a few years later. Work was only resumed in the 1920s . . . see F. Versteijnen C. S. Sp. *The Catholic Mission of Bagamoyo* (1968) section under heading: 25-4-1938. *Preliminary Notes*.

[29] Bishop Streicher's *imprimatur*, given at Villa Maria, is dated August 1911. This must have been one of the first books to be printed on the press at Bukalasa. The press remained there until its removal to Kisubi in 1938.

[30] Father Le Veux first joined the minor seminary staff in October 1903 at the move to Bukalasa. He had then just arrived from Europe. His great work, the *Premier essai de vocabulaire luganda-français* was printed at Maison Carrée in 1917. He had completed it in France in an ambulance unit at the front. It opens with an introductory letter from Mgr Livinhac, now near the end of his life. Over a thousand pages long, it has remained the basic work on Luganda vocabulary. Le Veux was rector of Bukalasa from July 1932 until August 1947. He died in January 1965 and is buried at Bukalasa.

Father Gorju was rector of Bukalasa from 1914 until 1919. He wrote several books, including the well-known *Entre le Victoria, l'Albert et l'Edouard* (1920), of value anthropologically. He was also the first editor of the Luganda newspaper *Munno*, begun in January 1911 and at that time printed at Bukalasa. Begun as a monthly it is now a daily. Gorju was appointed first vicar apostolic of Burundi in 1922, resigned in 1938 and died in December 1942. He returned to Uganda after his resignation and is also buried at Bukalasa.

that of Bukalasa and Katigondo.[31] The six year minor
seminary course was followed by nine further years before
ordination, including two of actual ministry, and yet the
first two Baganda priests were ordained in 1913. By 1924
seventeen men had been ordained and a few years later—
by the early thirties—a systematic policy of handing over
the parishes of the Masaka district was begun. From 1934
pastoral work in Masaka district was wholly in African
hands.[32] In 1939 this became a separate vicariate under the
first African Catholic bishop of modern times, Joseph
Kiwanuka.[33] By then 73 priests—not all of them, of course,
Baganda—had been ordained from Katigondo. The calibre
of this first generation of African priests was, I think, very
impressive. The very length and quality of the education
offered (in comparison with anything available elsewhere)
helped to encourage the best. Many of these older Baganda
priests worked for years outside Buganda, and some indeed
are still there—in Kigezi and Ankole. Devoted pastors,
conscientious administrators (like Mgr Maurice Mukasa,
Bishop Kiwanuka's vicar general for many years), scholars
and linguists (like the historian Father Joseph Ddiba), they
represent the specific response of a second generation of
christians to the responsibility of sharing in the church's life
and ministry.[34] They were supported by a growing number
of local religious brothers—the *Bannakaroli*.

31 See the significant comments in the *Phelps-Stokes Report*, p. 161.
Their visit was in March 1924.

32 In 1934 an African vicar delegate (Fr Joseph Mpagi) was placed in
general authority over all the Masaka parishes. The first African parish
priest of Villa Maria itself, Fr Maurice Mukasa (ordained like Fr
Mpagi in 1924) was installed by Fr LeVeux November 1 1934 (*Diary
of Katigondo*).

33 The telegram announcing his appointment arrived June 1 1939
(*Diary of Katigondo*). Bishop Kiwanuka had been ordained ten years
earlier, in 1929. He had since joined the White Fathers Society, studied
in Rome, and then returned—first to parish work, then to teach at
Katigondo. After more than twenty years as bishop in Masaka, he
became archbishop of Rubaga in 1960, attended all the sessions of the
Vatican Council, and died in February 1966.

34 Fr Ddiba was ordained in 1925. His two-volume history, *Eddini*

There is undoubtedly a dynamism and a determination in this movement, both from the missionary side and in the African response, that is very impressive; from the establishment of the first seminary through the ordination of the first priests and on to the consecration of the first bishop forty years later. Given the conditions of the system, it surely could not have been done faster. And, if this was indeed fully consistent with White Father policy elsewhere, as with that of *Propaganda Fide*, it is still true that its outstanding success here was largely due to the personal determination of Bishop Streicher and his closest collaborators.

A further field of work should also be noted, and surely a remarkable one: the establishment of an order of African sisters. This work began with the recruiting of female catechists in 1904. Out of this group, under the formation of White Sisters, and especially Mother Mechtilde, there developed the Congregation of the Daughters of Mary, *Bannabikira*. The first eleven took a promise of obedience and chastity in 1910. In August 1925 it was officially constituted as a diocesan congregation, when 130 sisters took permanent vows at the same moment and elected their own general superior. This very rapid development of female cooperation in church work is, in the African context, in some ways the most remarkable of all Streicher's achievements.

It should be noted that in the 1920s the *Bannabikira* were joined by a second congregation—the 'Little Sisters of St Francis'—based at Nkokonjeru, within the Mill Hill vicariate in the eastern part of Buganda. Begun on African initiative—the idea came from a girl called Pauline Musenero—a first group was formed in 1923 under the guidance of Mother Kevin of the Franciscan Missionaries for Africa. The first vows were taken in August 1928.

If we now compare the work of the two missions in these

---

mu Uganda, was published at Masaka in 1965 and 1967. Mgr Maurice Mukasa, Mgr Mpagi, Fr Ddiba and others of their generation are still alive, active church workers today.

years from the point of view of the extent to which they
maintained and developed an active and not just a passive
local church, we can say that for the laity the Anglican
Church, though not perfect, seems better than the Catholic.
The great Catholic chiefs did indeed take a very real part in
church life; on several occasions Stanislaus Mugwanya stood
out boldly in the Lukiko for the Catholic point of view and
the moral example and stern leadership provided by Alexis,
the county chief of Buddu, for so many years was surely a
source of inspiration for thousands.[35] How much the success
of missionary work depended upon the support and cooperation of such men is not perhaps always recognised.
The activity of the numerous body of catechists is also extremely impressive, but at the level of parish and inter-
parochial decision-making it was only after the second world
war that Bishop Kiwanuka developed in Masaka parish
councils and parents' associations in a way that has since
been copied by other dioceses.

Here, however, one can still insert a proviso. The strength

35 Alexis Sebbowa is a man who deserves a far more extensive study
than he has received. Already a sub-chief before the persecutions, he
had become by 1890 *Sekibobo*—county chief of Kyagwe—and one of
the greatest lords in the land. In the 1892 reshuffle he exchanged offices
with Sebwato and became *Pokino*; he ruled Buddu with great authority
for many decades. Lugard's Diaries are filled with his praises, for
instance the following: 'The Sekibobo has perhaps done more than any
man in the country to assist us. He was not in the fighting against us.
He brought back the king. He is a man in whom I have *absolute* confidence, and whom I personally like very much. The Protestants trust
him completely . . .' April 5 1892 (III, p. 145). See also Lugard's *The
Rise of Our East African Empire* (W. Blackwood & Sons, 1893),
especially II, pp. 375–377. He remained county chief of Buddu for
over thirty years and died in September 1937. Bwanda, the first house
and generalate of the *Bannabikira*, to date the largest order of African
nuns in the Church, is land given by him personally. He lies buried
beside his great house at Kyojjomanyi, not far away. When in May
1935 Fr Dupupet, the rector of Katigondo, had an accident and needed
to be quickly transported to the capital, the diarist records: 'Alexis ex-
Pokino a eu l'aimabilité de prêter son automobile'. Two years later it
was Fr Dupupet who ministered at the burial at Kyojjomanyi (*Diary of
Katigondo*, entries for May 23 and 24 1935 and September 21 1937).

of the early Anglican system was its extremely close linking
of church and state implied in the concurrent responsibilities of the same men in both. County chiefs could become deacons, while the *katikiro* (prime minister) took an
interest in the spread of evangelism beyond the borders of
Buganda whose motivation was surely not purely religious.
Such a system certainly appealed to the Baganda and it
enabled the establishment of a structured local church to go
forward rapidly.[36] But as a system it certainly had very
serious weaknesses, inherent in every attempt to build the
church closely into the state, which appeared in subsequent
decades. The very dependence of church life upon the chiefs
meant that when, as happened in the next generation, there
were few chiefs of outstanding christian calibre, the life of
the church suffered greatly. The moral defection of a chief
could have deeper effects in the Anglican system than in the
Catholic.[37] Again, there was soon a very real danger—and

[36] Nevertheless it must not be forgotten that there *was* an understood
division between responsibility in church and state, even in the lay
sphere, almost from the start. This can be illustrated by a passing re-
mark of Ashe: 'Old Nikodemo, the Pokino of Buddu, showed some
annoyance at receiving orders from Kagwa, since Kagwa was nothing in
the *Church*, where he himself was the principal man' (R. Ashe,
Chronicles of Uganda, Hodder and Stoughton, 1894, pp. 141–142). This
refers back to 1891 when Nikodemo Sebwato was still *Pokino*. Sebwato's
death in March 1895 was certainly a grievous blow for the Anglican
Church. There was probably no one else on the Anglican side with
quite the stature of Kagwa (except for Kakunguru who had gone East),
and Kagwa was basically more of the politique than the churchman.
Indeed in many ways his position and outlook was very comparable
with that of his predecessor (not immediate, of course) the old pagan
katikiro, Mukasa. Each succeeded in maintaining his office across a
change of king; each had a ruthless personal grip upon political power
together with a very real sense of traditional Ganda values.
   Certainly after Sebwato's death Kagwa tended to take for granted his
own leadership in the church as well as the state. See, for instance, his
calling 'a meeting of the chiefs and more prominent christians' to plan
the building of a new cathedral in 1901 (Tucker, *Eighteen Years*, II,
p. 283).
   [37] By this contrast of 'system' I mean here, of course, a contrast as it
actually came to exist in Uganda. It was not a contrast in desire. The
Catholics would have been just as happy to have achieved an 'establish-

more than a danger—of a political churchmanship and of the tying of the church to the support of a political estab-lishment. It cannot be doubted that the 1966 political revolution in Buganda has, as a result, caused a rather serious disorientation in Protestant church life. The shock effect of this may well, of course, be followed by a very real re-awakening and sense of liberation; and the real life of the Anglican Church has anyway for long been carried forward by the Revival Movement rather than by the establishment.

Nevertheless it must be admitted that the Anglican Church in Buganda is today somehow paying for its privi-leged position obtained seventy years back, and for that very relationship between church leadership and chiefly leader-ship which initially allowed Anglican African laity to take such an active part in church life. So often can the very strength of one generation prove a source of weakness for the next!

All this may help to explain too the fact that whereas in the Catholic Church in Uganda its Buganda section still somehow retains today much of the leadership it held at the start, in the National Anglican Church the Buganda dioceses have undoubtedly declined in vigour and most leadership now comes from the West—Ankole, Kigezi and Toro.

As regards the ordained ministry it is still less easy to judge between the policy of the two communions. In, say, 1905 the detached observer would surely have concluded that the Anglican system was a far wiser one, the Catholic rigid, unadapted and hardly likely to succeed.[38] I would

---

ment', indeed they struggled hard to do so. It was in fact implicit in the whole concept of 'the christian kingdom' which was so central to Lavigerie's missionary theory.

[38] After writing the above I happened to come across a relevant re-mark of C. W. Hattersley written at just about the time I speak of. Hattersley was not, it is true, a 'detached observer' but a Protestant missionary with a decidedly jaundiced view of Roman Catholics. Never-theless his opinion was surely a common one. His book *The Baganda at Home* was first published in 1908 (reprinted, Frank Cass and Company, 1968). Speaking of the Catholic Church he says (p. 220):

tend to agree with this myself, and yet in some ways results do not confirm such a judgment. It is to be noted that when a profession and its traditions are established, the first pattern can prove difficult to change later on. The rather low level of education which became the norm for Anglican priests at the beginning has become a major problem sixty years later, providing an image of the clergy in a developing country which has slight attraction for the younger generation. The rather high academic level insisted on by the Catholics at the beginning, even if its content was far too formal and scholastic, has resulted sixty years later in the Catholic priesthood being by and large very much better equipped intellectually to deal with Uganda's modern society. And even in numbers in Buganda the Catholic clergy do not today lag behind. Adaptation has, after all, to be made with an eye to the future as well as to the present.

It is, however, most certainly true that a system of training which on the whole can be said to have succeeded in Buganda and to have helped create today a rather strong church has not worked out comparably elsewhere. For whatever reason the Eastern and Northern Regions, for instance, give a very different impression, and it would not be easy to maintain that in those areas the Catholic system has worked out better than the Protestant. Further, it can be added that the fault in the Anglican system surely lay not in the start of the ministry in Bishop Tucker's time but in a failure to adjust it sufficiently imaginatively in the thirty years following 1910, to keep in line (especially after the publication of the second *Phelps-Stokes Report*) with the quickly developing educational system of the country as a whole.

Bishop Tucker resigned in 1911 and one certainly has the impression that in the next forty years there was less sense of urgency among Anglicans in establishing a full local church, even though Tucker's successor, Bishop Willis, was

'They have no native clergy connected with their mission, and are not likely to have any unless they can remove the obstacle of celibacy.'

in some ways far closer to Africans, having a linguistic knowledge which Tucker never acquired. A situation in which the top levels of the ministry were confined to expatriate clergy came to be accepted as a quasi-permanent one. One feels that the minor schisms from the Anglican Church of the *Bamalaki* (beginning 1914) and that in the 1920s which resulted in the Orthodox Church of Uganda, and even the Revival Movement starting in the 1930s, all express something of a justified dissatisfaction within the Protestant Church with the degree in which the church had remained a 'Mission'.[39] The most significant institutional work in both churches in the decades following 1920 probably lay in their fine development of secondary schools for the laity.

The Revival Movement (*Balokole*), whose influence has clearly been of exceptional importance within the Anglican Church in the last thirty years, does however present a quite new element. It is one that cannot as such be paralleled on the Catholic side, though some comparison with the growth of local religious orders and even of the Legion of Mary— particularly from the viewpoint of providing scope for committed female fervour—could be sustained.

The Revival Movement grew widespread in 1937.[40] Its strength has been its predominantly African leadership and inspiration,[41] its largely lay character, and its continuance— despite tensions—within the original communion. It was both a reaction to the continued expatriate control of church life and the rather heavy character of an establishment

[39] See F. Welbourn, *East African Rebels*, London (SCM Press) 1961, part II, in particular quotations on pages 40, 84, 86.

[40] For the East African Revival Movement the best general study is Max Warren's *Revival, an Enquiry*, 1954; see also Taylor, op. cit., pp. 99–105, 223–226, and Welbourn, op. cit., pp. 72–75. For its development in western Kenya reference should be made to F. Welbourn and B. Ogot, *A Place to Feel at Home*, part II.

[41] The Revival was however clearly influenced in its stress both on fellowship and on the public confession of sins by the contemporary 'Oxford Group' movement (subsequently known as MRA).

religion, and yet at the same time a renewal of that very religion from within. The missionary journeys of African 'Revival Teams' to Kenya and Tanganyika recall the missionary fervour of an earlier generation of Baganda. A Masaka shopkeeper, Crisafati Matovu, converted by some revivalists who spent a night with him in the late 1930s, set off for Buha in western Tanganyika where he worked for many years as an evangelist, later becoming a priest and rural dean. As an originally African movement which has yet not broken into schism, the East African Revival does indeed remain almost unique, and credit here must be given to its very understanding handling by Bishop Stuart, the successor of Willis. The whole thing witnesses to the continued vigour of response to the gospel in a third generation. It may well be that the much greater extensiveness of Roman Catholic expatriate missionary activity in the last thirty years is the decisive reason why nothing quite comparable on the native side has happened within the Catholic communion.

Just because the Catholic procedure was such that it could only come to a peak more slowly, so too the specifically missionary momentum lasted longer.[42] But there is a clear impression that other bishops were far less effectively preoccupied than Streicher with the establishment of a viable local church, and that the Masaka area was a far too complete exception to the normal pattern. Here again, a mission situation was more or less accepted as quasi-permanent. Until well into the 1950s it was taken for granted that missionaries should retire up or to the side but could not (unless in exceptional cases and with very special safeguards) remain on *beneath* African superiors within an African church. Such an attitude—still apparent in some places—

---

[42] This can, of course, be partly explained too in terms of the steady increase in the number of Catholic missionary personnel, decade after decade, while the Anglican expatriate mission force ceased to grow after about 1920 and then came to decrease. Compare the 1904 figures Taylor gives with those for 1926 (op. cit., pp. 71 and 92–93).

immensely retards the work of establishing a local church. Bishop Kiwanuka remained the sole African Catholic bishop in Uganda for over twenty years, until in fact, with his elevation to the archiepiscopal see of Rubaga in December 1960, his successor in the diocese of Masaka, Mgr Adrian Ddungu, was appointed the following year. Only in October 1968 was the first African diocesan bishop in the Northern and Eastern regions consecrated (Mgr Asili of Lira). He has, however, been rapidly followed by two further diocesan bishops in those parts.

In the Anglican Church too a large scale africanisation of the episcopate only came in the 1960s. A number of African diocesan bishops were appointed after the establishment of the Province early in 1961 and an African metropolitan, Archbishop Sabiti of Fort Portal, Toro, elected in January 1966 to succeed Archbishop Brown. Today a sole European bishop remains in the Church of Uganda, and he was elected by the diocese concerned.

VI

The deep similarities in the development of the two churches within Buganda are clear. Both were hierarchical and it cannot be doubted that their solid establishment was assisted by the hierarchical character of traditional Ganda society. Their early pattern of organisation, their use of numerous catechists, their concern with the development of a local clergy, their educational systems at primary and secondary level, their africanisation of the hierarchy in the last ten years—in many points their development has been a parallel one.

On the other hand, as we have already seen, there have also been considerable differences which it may here be useful to summarise. The first has been a consistently different approach to the training and character of the ordained clergy (though the difference in training today is considerably less than it ever was in the past). A second has been a

different relationship to political authority. This was more
noticeable in Buganda than in most parts of British Africa
because the tie-up here was not only between British rule
and the Anglican communion which was of a very restrained
kind, but still more between the local Anglican Church and
the Ganda monarchy and dominant political group. It was
this that gave the former a very particular establishment
character in Buganda with both its strength and its weaknesses. However, it should not be forgotten that on a much
smaller scale something similar operated to the advantage of
Catholics in the great county of Buddu, especially during
the earlier years while Alexis was county chief. His behaviour was that of a semi-independent ruler. But his suc-
cessors had not the same authority; the importance of the
position of Pokino has steadily decreased throughout the
century.

Thirdly, the growing difference in the number of foreign
missionaries of the two communions has undoubtedly been
a major factor. Up to about 1920 there was a rough parity.
Since then the Anglican missionary force has quietly declined, while the Catholics steadily increased until about
1960. With this has gone the kind of work they do. For years
no Anglican missionary has been engaged in permanent
pastoral work in the countryside while many Catholic missionaries are still so engaged today. Mitala Maria, for instance, an important mission-parish forty miles west of
Kampala, was founded in 1899. In 1969 it was still staffed by
foreign White Fathers.

Fourthly, the Revival Movement in the Anglican Church
and the widespread development of indigenous religious
orders (together with local vocations to some older religious
societies, such as the Brothers of Christian Instruction) in
the Catholic Church represent strongly different approaches
to the rejuvenating and enriching of christian life in a
church entering its second half century.

Lastly, the Anglican Church was built upon a close knowledge of scripture such as the Catholics never had. The

Anglican Luganda Bible was first completed in 1896; it has since been revised. The Catholics had the gospels from the last century and in recent times have possessed a complete New Testament, but even now they have no Luganda Old Testament. Nor do they make any extensive use of the Protestant translation. On the other hand Catholic life has been a strongly sacramental one, while even now Anglicans in Uganda do not consider Holy Communion to be the normal Sunday service. Sacramental confession and communion have surely been the great force for holiness among Baganda Catholics.

VII

Perhaps today the most relevant aspects of the mission-church relationship are financial and cultural; we cannot tackle the vast problems that these involve here, vital as they are. The cultural problem can be particularly subtle in young churches such as that of Buganda, which already have some sixty or more years of settled history and a quite recognisable pattern of local church life. European devotional attitudes of the late 19th century (both Catholic and Protestant) are now very deeply built into local christianity.[43] Today, such attitudes (often repudiated by modern European christians, but maybe held to tenaciously by African christians especially of the older generation) cannot easily be classified as either 'European' or 'African'. After all, cultural assimilation does not follow a priori rules. When an African priest stands by the harmonium and the use of Latin, while an expatriate presses for the liturgical use of drums and the vernacular, the cultural shape of the mission-local church encounter is not easy to delineate.[44]

43 For an interesting study of how nineteenth century Evangelicalism has survived in the twentieth century Church of Uganda see John Poulton, *Like Father, Like Son*, Some Reflections on the Church of Uganda, *International Review of Missions*, 1961, pp. 297–307.

44 Of course in many places today young Africans prefer neither harmonium nor drum but a guitar.

From the financial point of view the pre-1920 period could provide an excellent example. The mission was then largely self-supporting and the local church was taught to be the same.[45] Churches were constructed in local materials at little cost, the missionaries lived on their own garden produce. Today the pattern is, unfortunately, often a different one. The desire to emulate the costly buildings and institutions of Europe and North America forces the African Church, entirely lacking in adequate resources for such a feat, to become a permanent beggar. And he who pays the piper can and will, to a considerable extent, call the tune. Once again, this is a far more serious problem for the Catholic Church, because it seems in fact to be able to obtain more considerable funds elsewhere. The Anglican Church maintains a more consistent policy of self-reliance.[46] It will certainly be increasingly important in the future for the churches—if they wish to be true self-ministering, self-supporting communities—to scrutinise very exactly their use of foreign money.

I have tried in this survey to present the ebb and flow of events over ninety lively years of church history. We have seen something of how the forces of mission control and local initiative have pressed upon each other, sometimes in one form, sometimes in another. It is clear, of course, that there must be some missionary control in the early days of a new church and plenty of instances elsewhere can show how a local church too quickly left on its own may either go strange ways, disintegrate, or—most likely of all—fall into a very conservative groove, a static maintenance of the original, necessarily rather simple, pattern.

There is, it is clear, no simple formula for church building, for the development of an adequate local ministry, for

[45] See Tucker's interesting remarks on the subject, *Eighteen Years*, I, pp. 358–359.

[46] The stress on this in *The Ten Year Plan*, dated March 1967, of the Church of Uganda, Rwanda and Burundi (printed by the Uganda Bookshop) is quite clear.

the structuring of lay initiative, for the establishment of just such institutions as are inherently viable within a given economy, for the whole relationship between a sending and a young church. All this becomes still more complex when the wider context is one of rather rapid social change. The Holy Spirit, as the human temperament also and different historic christian traditions, can lead many ways. Certainly from many points of view early missionary work in Buganda stands out as a model which could have been happily imitated elsewhere. Yet even here one feels that in both communions, though faced with this quite exceptionally vigorous response from people some of whom were of clearly outstanding character, the missionaries were often too slow to trust the young christians fully, or at least too tied by the institutional ways and acquired reflexes they had brought from home.

On the other hand it is clear too that there were many missionaries at work here of exceptional ability and fervour and their basic aims cannot be called in question, nor indeed the soundness of most of the work achieved. Certainly time and again in Buganda the quality of the missionaries and that of the young christians have balanced one another. One and the other have, with the grace of God, worked to establish a tradition of christian living and a church community whose essential viability can hardly today be called in question. There is a tendency nowadays to suggest that a vigorous African response to christianity is only to be found in the break-away independent churches. I think it should be clear that in Buganda at least this is very far from true. I have tried to illustrate the quality of the African response within the historic churches for the first generation of converts in the 1880s, which included both the martyrs and the subsequent lay readers of the church; for a second generation of men coming to maturity about the turn of the century, and for a third generation represented both by the growing group of educated Catholic priests ordained in the 1920s and 30s and the leaders of the Revival. The same could be shown for subsequent generations—for many men, laity and priests, who came to the front rank in the years of rapid expansion after the second world war. And it is, I am convinced, true again of those coming forward in the 1960s.

The church exists. But that is always only a beginning. If the 'mission' was for the church, so is the church for mission. The really important questions today are not, 'Is there a local hierarchy? Can the church survive? Is its internal organisation as efficient as when it was mostly in missionary hands?' but instead, 'Is this new church continuing to be a missionary church? Does it as a human community have a sense of service rather than of self-preservation? Is its life half as vital in the new urban areas as in the old rural ones? Does it retain any effective commitment among the growing group of graduates? Is its ordained ministry succumbing to the temptations of clericalism? Do its rich members help its poor ones? Is it evangelically self-critical? Does it challenge secular society, speaking out for the poor and the oppressed?' Such are the questions that the church in Buganda should be asking itself today.

11

NEW HORIZONS FOR THE CHURCH IN TANZANIA

The church in Tanzania is a young church fast becoming a mature one. With a hundred years of history, well over two million members, nearly 500 local priests and 1,500 local sisters, it is a church with substance to it. The great majority of its twenty-three dioceses are now led by Tanzanian bishops. It is a church which one can envisage surviving the total withdrawal of overseas aid and personnel without complete disruption. It is quite probable that it stands in a stronger position that does the Catholic Church in any other country of Africa today.

Again it is a church relatively well integrated into the life of the nation. Catholics participate naturally in this at all levels without any undue complexes, either of superiority or of exclusion. Relations with other christian bodies are generally harmonious, and even with regard to Islam there is probably less tension than in other African countries with a comparable Moslem population. The church in Tanzania has given birth to a fair range of institutions, from primary and secondary schools to four major seminaries, the Social Training Centre at Nyegezi, the printing presses at Kipalapala and Ndanda, the Kiongozi newspaper, but without appearing to be putting forward some rival institutional system to that of the nation as a whole. These are general remarks which would require modification in regard to certain areas: for instance, political participation was slow in coming and is even now (apart from the president) quite inadequate at the most senior level. Moreover, it is in general in some of the more remote dioceses that national and ecclesiastical integration has been best achieved—in the sense that the church as institution does not appear to be something strikingly foreign.

Certainly in the church of Tanzania there is much to look back upon with reasonable content, but there is still more to look forward to. The existing system does not in fact offer of itself a continuing viable pattern for the coming years, for it included—and still includes—a degree of overseas dependence neither practical nor desirable; it was also deeply related structurally and mentally to the pre-nationalist world of colonialism. Nevertheless what has been accomplished in Tanzania does offer—what some other churches in Africa more notably lack—a reasonable springboard for the growth and adaptation of the years ahead.

Today Tanzania is being swept by the winds of the cultural revolution. Led by its president, a particularly sincere church member, it is committed by the Arusha Declaration and the developing concept of 'Ujamaa' to the bringing into being of an essentially free and peaceful socialist society, characterised by the best of traditional African collectivism, growing out of the extended family and the village community, reinterpreted in the context of an inter-tribal modern nation state. If there is any policy which the church of *Gaudium et Spes* and *Populorum Progressio* should encourage and support, it is surely this. At the same time there are, admittedly, two sources of trouble. At a low level there are plenty of local officials who understand very little of what it is all about and they are often not properly controlled. At a high level there are the pressures of international power politics and the real danger of Tanzania's internal development being stunted by the requirements of foreign policy. The government's correct conviction that it could have an important part to play in the liberation of southern Africa could, all the same, lead not to that but to its own partial subjection to overseas communist forces; of this the government itself is, of course, well aware. It is a duty for the institutional church to be sufficiently politically conscious and outspoken to try and ensure that the national commitment to the wider freedom struggle does not in fact involve a continual diminishing of internal freedom.

In taking stock of itself and its future a local church needs to consider, first, its structures; second, and still more important, its evangelical effectiveness; third, its social involvement. The three are, of course, continuously intertwined; and all require a correct basic stance. Both intrinsic ecclesial exigencies and the facts of the contemporary situation call on the church in Tanzania today to be in full measure a 'church' and not a 'mission'—yet a church with a mission. The church is the sacrament of salvation, and the local church must be the sign of salvation within its own context: an adapted, convincing bearer of the christian gospel within and to a particular group of men with their own cultural, regional characteristics. It can only be this if it takes its calling as a local church really seriously and equips itself for this with suitable mechanisms. In the end only those on the spot can suitably judge what those should be in the fields of worship, ministry, service. That is why it is necessary that churches both in the East and in the West 'fully enjoy the right, and are in duty bound, to rule themselves'. (Decree on Eastern Catholic Churches, n. 5.)

Tanzania is a very special country. For one thing it has a particularly rural character. Almost no country of comparable importance in Africa is so little urbanised. Hence, already, it should be clear that the institutional needs of its church are likely to be at quite the other end of the spectrum from those of the most influential European and North American lands, all of which are particularly concerned at present with witness and service within the urban, industrial context. This side of society cannot be neglected in Tanzania and the needs of Dar es Salaam have a quite particular importance. It is a very fast growing city. The very fact that there is no other large town in Tanzania, combined with the great distances and poor communications characteristic of the country as a whole, combine in giving Dar a quite special significance in the life of the nation as a whole: the centre of government, the one big industrial area, the sole university. Moreover here as elsewhere the 1970s will be a period of spectacular urban growth. From the Catholic point of view it has to be added that the church is not well structured here. The traditionally Moslem character of the coast which, at least in the town, is now passing; the almost complete absence of local priests in this part of the country; the very particular problems in the development of a strong church community among a still very unstable urban population: these and other factors all contribute to make of Dar es Salaam the biggest single challenge facing the church of Tanzania. It is a challenge that can only be faced at national level but also only in largely lay terms, in the stimulation of new types of christian community. Nevertheless far more African priests are needed here, especially perhaps for the peri-urban areas where the population is also rapidly growing with immigrants from inland but where at present parishes are almost non-existent.

Nevertheless the balance in the whole country is, and will probably long remain, very much on the rural side and also very much on the poor side. Tanzania, unlike—for example —Zambia, has no quick way to wealth. The government of Tanzania has accepted this fact very frankly indeed, and its whole basic policy as expressed in the Arusha Declaration and related documents is to develop Tanzania in a realistic way, geared to its own inherent potentialities and limitations rather than to imitating societies with very different potentialities. A healthy church must follow the same pattern. It is strictly necessary that if the church in Tanzania is to be truly the local church of Tanzania and not the 'mission extension' of European and North American churches, it accept the central insight contained in the

Arusha Declaration not simply as normative for the country's national policy, but also for its own internal structuring.

This is necessary at the level of planning, whether it concern the shape of the ministry, liturgical revision or the content of seminary training; it is necessary at the level of personnel (it is impossible for the ministry of a healthy self-reliant local church to be predominantly recruited from abroad); it is necessary at the level of finance—the local church of Tanzania must not be a church whose financial support is largely derived from overseas. Certainly the church in Tanzania today has a long way to go from all these three points of view.

To take first the matter of full-time personnel. It would seem to be impossible for a local church to shape itself effectively, to grow with the nation, to make its specific witness felt, while the majority of its ministers, planners and spokesmen are foreigners—as is the case for priests today. The balance in 1970 is about 65% foreign to 35% indigenous. (Note that the balance of sisters is already 40:60, the other way round.) A situation of this sort is inevitable in the early stages of a missionary church, but after one hundred years it should not still exist. A young church can continue to claim some substantial help from outside but this help should not be such as to replace or limit its own predominating activities. Probably not more than 20% of full-time church personnel can suitably be expatriate in the sort of situation the church of Tanzania has now reached.

The balance is, in fact, changing every year. The missionary force is already decreasing and its advanced average age in many places ensures that further decrease in the coming years will be marked. The local clergy and local sisterhoods are considerably on the increase. It may be that no drastic efforts will be needed to achieve a far more satisfactory balance within a shortish term of years. What is essential, though, is that this should be seen to be good;

no tears should be lost over the decrease of missionary personnel, and no frantic efforts should be made to bring this to a halt. We should instead plot a clear graph for the future, aiming at a 50:50 clergy ratio by 1975, a 60:40 position before 1980, and then a fairly rapid movement towards an 80:20 position. It is quite likely that the government itself will not be prepared to tolerate a larger expatriate force than that by the 1980s. The recognition of this pattern for the future must, of course, lead to a clear quota system for both dioceses and special institutions. The decreasing missionary force must increasingly be directed towards the particular areas of work which it can still properly make its own. I would suggest that these are two: one, areas of the country where evangelisation has still recently begun; two, certain specialised functions especially within training institutions (though, of course, neither of these areas belongs to expatriate workers exclusively). Furthermore, to maintain the sense of Catholic communion within the local church, it can reasonably be urged that a rather small group of expatriate clergy (doubtless, for the most part, older men) could profitably remain for a time in other dioceses, working side by side with local clergy.

From whatever point of view it is considered, an efficient use of expatriate staff in these circumstances seems impossible while institutes continue to be linked with a sole diocese or part of the country.

A first corollary to this view of the future of the expatriate clergy must, of course, be one of a very large increase in local ministry. At present there may be, on average, some twenty-five new Tanzanian priests a year. This is good in comparison with most African countries, but it remains quite inadequate for the needs of Tanzania. There is already a great strain upon the pastoral and missionary ministry in many areas, and with a continuing increase of Catholic population (5–6% a year) and a decline in missionaries, it is perfectly clear that the basic needs of the church cannot possibly be met in the future with the present pattern of ministry and recruitment of it.

One of the most practical expedients would be to engage sisters in far more general pastoral work than they are doing at present. This is particularly feasible as Tanzania has already a rather large number of local sisters. There is no sound reason why a large part of a priest's activities should not be taken over where necessary by sisters, even with absolute gain, and one of the most important immediate tasks facing the church in Tanzania is surely an exact survey of the present work and future potentialities of local sisters.

By itself, however, this expedient can hardly have a decisive effect with regard to the needs of outlying areas in large parishes. Tanzania is a particularly large and, in most regions, sparsely populated country. Its communications are also notoriously bad, at least during the rainy months. In almost all parts of the country there are numerous parishes with outstations fifty miles and more away from the centre. Hence, even more than in the neighbouring countries of Kenya and Uganda, there is an urgent need to re-examine the needs and possibilities of local village ministry. Tanzania has already a relatively large number of catechist training centres. It seems urgently necessary to develop them, or some among them, as institutions providing ministers with a wider range of functions than have the traditional catechists. Deacons are very much the first step and it is high time that they were more than talked about. The most important single step facing the Tanzanian church precisely now from the side of ministry is to start seriously and extensively with the recruitment and training of married deacons.

Nevertheless, neither sisters nor deacons can provide the mass and they cannot therefore substitute for an ordained priest from this decisive point of view of making possible the focal action of a local eucharistic community. Without this all else can fall apart. In rural areas where the

7

traditional type of priest can only seldom visit, there is a particularly obvious need for making some married deacons into priests. There can be no doubt whatever this is going to come. The only question is whether, when it comes, it will already be too late to catch up with the backlog of communities already declining in fervour because they have been systematically starved of the sacraments and deprived of a viable church structure.

A considerable proportion of the priests now being ordained are sent for further studies either in Dar es Salaam or abroad. This is a recognition of the undoubted fact that there are a growing number of specialised ministries, that the major seminaries should be in large part staffed by qualified local personnel, and that there should also be priests able to participate in university teaching. We have a very long way to go in this direction. It is essential that the local church should aim at having more than a handful of men with not only a first, but a second, degree, able to stand level with the new class of super-graduates, to plan church work on a wide scale, and to offer a genuinely Tanzanian contribution to christian thought. Some young men recently ordained or soon to be ordained have to be sent to achieve this sort of standard. Evidently time and expense are involved in this. Five years of full-time study for someone who has already gained a good Higher Certificate and completed his basic theological course may be a minimum, but the local church cannot afford to recruit its experts chiefly from foreigners (even if it could get them) and the standard of expertise in the modern world is continually rising.

However much the shape of the ordained ministry may be adapted in the coming years, the strength of the church in Tanzania does already, and will increasingly, depend upon the strength of its laity. There can be no doubt about this, whether one considers the town life of Dar es Salaam, the country life of countless remote villages, the academic life of the university or the teaching and practice of religion in primary and secondary schools. The fact is clear, the question remains as to how best enable the laity embrace its responsibilities effectively, how to incorporate them adequately into the processes of church decision-making, and to ensure that church membership is a stimulus to participation in the various aspects of national life. Firstly, there needs to be a great increase in retreats, conferences and refresher courses, and both centres and funds for such are required. Again, it must be ensured that the coming recruitment from married men for an extensive diaconate is a means to strengthen the lay apostolate and not the removal of the lay cream to join the clerical segment in an inferior role. A real value of the diaconate could be exactly as a bridge between lay and clerical workers. Further, the reality of lay co-responsibility will be guaranteed by the effectiveness of diocesan pastoral councils and parish councils. It would be desirable that laymen should be present too at the national meetings of bishops. It should not be suggested that there is any general field of church work where lay interest and participation is not a gain. The future of the church depends at least as much on a radical laicisation of functions and responsibilities as on a restructuring of clerical ministry.

Outside help may continue to reach the church of Tanzania in considerable quantities for many years to come, but from any point of view it would be criminal to take it for granted that this will in fact be so. The aim of policy must be to achieve as great as possible a measure of self-reliance by 1980 at the latest. Here the question of money obviously arises. It is perfectly reasonable that certain special institutions and projects should be supported financially from abroad, especially if they are such as the government would be likely to wish to take over if the church were no longer able to maintain them. It is quite another matter to envisage an indefinite continuance of the system operating at present in most parts, whereby the basic requirements for the ordinary pastoral ministry—even in areas long since extensively evangelised—are largely met with outside money. This obviously applies particularly to the maintenance of parishes and the salaries of catechists. Financial self-reliance is not only practically useful for a church; it is also theologically required that a properly established local church be a viable economic unit. The people of God locally gathered must, like other groups of people, express this commitment in part in a financial way.

This has, of course, been strongly insisted upon in many places. The point here is that financial self-reliance is simply unconvincing if it is not pretty complete. It is hard to convince village christians that their local church must be self-reliant, if the parish itself is manifestly not so. It is hard to convince a parish of the same thing, if—within the one diocese—a cathedral is being built at vast expense with foreign funds. Financial self-reliance has, of its essence, to be a consistent policy; otherwise it simply becomes a mockery with the ecclesiastical 'haves' (those in touch with foreign sources) telling the 'have nots' to feed themselves.

If the church in Tanzania must be increasingly self-reliant both as regards personnel and as regards finance, it can certainly only do this if it thinks far more in national, and less in diocesan or tribal terms, than hitherto. The disproportion in financial resources between different dioceses is quite obvious and highly undesirable. There is also a failure to pool priests and sisters except in rather special cases. Up till now the weight of decision-making with regard to both men and money has been at diocesan level. This was a corollary of a 'mission' situation in which dioceses were tied to various missionary institutes. If dioceses in Tanzania are now truly to form the church of Tanzania, this has to change very considerably and the decisive criterion must become relative local need, assessed in national terms, rather than the overseas contacts of particular dioceses. In this context particular attention and help needs to be given to the three or four clearly sub-standard dioceses which can hardly pull themselves up without particular help from elsewhere, as also to certain eastern areas where the church is still hardly present at all.

The church does not exist for herself but for witness and service. She cannot fulfil her function if her structures are seriously at variance with local needs, and structures have to be paid much attention to—especially when they have been shaped to so considerable an extent upon the type of church existing in western Europe. Nevertheless the church cannot be primarily concerned with her structures, and there is always a danger of church planning looking too much this way—perpetually reservicing the car but never actually going anywhere. The outgoing dimension must always take priority.

Inter-church relations in Tanzania have on the whole been fairly cordial. In some areas there was in the past a clash between two missionary groups, but in much of the country this has been avoided. Furthermore, almost everywhere relations have enormously improved in the last few years, including some of the places which previously had the worst record. On the whole, however, not much thought seems to be given today by Catholics to ecumenical activity. This is doubtless due in part to the problem of distances, but only in part and much could be done which is not as yet being done. Evidently there is a difference here between relations with the low church Anglican dioceses of the centre and North-West and the Lutheran and Moravian churches on the one hand, and the Anglican dioceses of the UMCA tradition on the other. Relations are increasingly cordial with the former, but it is not as yet possible with them to undertake the intimate liturgical and pastoral cooperation and to create a growing sense of being effectively one religious community, which is clearly possible and called for in southern and eastern areas where high church anglicanism is the only or chief other communion in the vicinity. It is probable that nowhere else in the world is there a better opportunity for full unity in our time between the Roman Catholic communion and one stemming

from the divisions of the sixteenth century. The chief difficulty here is the growing fear of church authorities, both
local and universal, of countenancing a movement to unity
at a regional level which is going significantly faster than
elsewhere in the country or the world.

Some things can be done for all christians in common.
Tanzania already possesses a common Swahili bible since
the wise acceptance by the Catholic authorities of the Union
Protestant version. That is real progress. Besides this, it is
of urgent importance for inter-church relations that all
adopt a common Swahili form for the basic christian
prayers: the Lord's prayer, the Apostles' and Nicene creeds,
the Gloria Patri, Kyrie, Gloria in excelsis, Sanctus and
Agnus Dei. Agreement with the Christian Council on this
relatively simple point should be gained as soon as possible.

The christian and Moslem communities are of roughly
equivalent size in Tanzania, and there is no strong tradition of hostility. Government policy has wisely stressed the
importance of social integration of the two. Throughout
Africa christian-Moslem relations present special problems
and in many places are bad and even growing worse. Tanzania has the opportunity of being an exception here and
in gripping the opportunity it could be doing a very considerable service to the world church and general world
harmony. But this cannot happen without positive effort,
and it would be desirable for several capable Tanzanian
priests and laymen to specialise in Islamic studies. Dialogue
and cooperation between christians and moslems could be
much helped by the establishment of a joint Department
of Religious Studies at Dar es Salaam University. Our
brotherhood of faith in the one living God should offer
witness to a world in which christians and moslems are
still too often bitterly divided.

The church of Tanzania is part of the world church. It
must be, beyond its own borders, a giving church, not
simply a receiving one: giving of inspiration, of commitment, and even of men. It must first of all be missionary at

home, and it is high time that the stronger Catholic groups —the Ngoni, the Bahaya, the Wafipa and the Wachaga— should be showing an effective concern for the more evidently missionary areas of the country. But the missionary thrust should also go further afield. 'Let them (the young churches) send their own missionaries out . . . even though they themselves are suffering from a shortage of clergy' (*Ad Gentes*, 20). Undoubtedly, the church of Tanzania is in a stronger position than many of its neighbours, and it may well be that in the coming years a Tanzanian mission will need to be sent forth to Zambia or Mozambique, to Kenya or the Sudan. These four large countries have between them far fewer local priests or local sisters than Tanzania has alone. Is one getting ready for such a venture? Are the leaders of the Tanzanian church sufficiently conscious of their responsibilities to the world beyond, and the church beyond? Are its bishops ready to take an active part in the world dialogue at present increasingly taking place within the episcopate?

The greatest question of all that the church in Tanzania must ask herself is: is her work really relevant to the daily lives and needs of the millions of Tanzanians? to the Sukuma cotton growers, to the Masai herdsmen, to the industrial workers of Dar es Salaam, to the new generation of students? Has she really got a message at all? That message has somehow to combine the uniqueness, harshness, universality of the gospel with the human needs of this society. Tanzania is economically a very poor society in comparison with many, but it is one particularly concentrated upon development and nation building: the creation of an egalitarian, predominantly Swahili speaking people, an Ujamaa society. As regards the whole social and political trend of the country, perhaps nowhere else in the third world is so serious and consistent an effort being made to build a socialist society by peaceful means. The goal is clear, the means often very much less so. It is for the local church to commit herself generously to the great aims and the spirit of the Arusha Declaration while retaining the freedom and showing the courage to point out injustices and inadequacies in its implementation. There is a danger here as in so many other countries of the church becoming a rubber stamp for the latest government policies. This is to be avoided not by opting out, but by a generous participation which is neither blind nor fearful.

Tanzania is one of the few countries of Africa which has fully adopted an African language as its official one and is making real efforts to develop it as an adequate vehicle for modern needs of communication. The church certainly has quite a good tradition in the use of Swahili, and the Swahili liturgy and its accompanying music is blossoming better than many all over the world, but far too little effort has been made (despite the church's two efficient printing presses) to develop an adequate Swahili literature in the fields of theology, spirituality and catechetics.

There is no doubt that the church is engaged in one way and another in many valuable development projects. As the years go by and the shape of civil society changes, these have to be seriously reviewed. The nationalisation of the schools must make the church both develop effective ways in the new situation of transmitting the gospel to the younger generation and find new forms of social involvement. Some of these will, of course, continue to be educational, but of a less managerial form. A new area of the greatest importance both for Tanzania and many other African countries is that of schemes of 'further education' and employment for the great majority of children for whom full-time schooling ends with the primary. The question always needs to be put anew: is enough being done for those who have been somehow left aside in the march of progress? The church should indeed help form an elite, but it must also have a special care for the lame dog, and for groups—whether tribal, regional, of age or intellectual ability—which are not getting a fair deal. The rather shabby treatment the Masai have received in Tanzania in the last few years is a case in point: nation-building should not mean the arbitrary and enforced destruction of a sub-group's distinguishing characteristics. Manifest concern for such things is a mission which has always to be shouldered anew by 'the church of the poor'. But across every particular form of service it has to proclaim in comprehensible and challenging terms the one gospel of Christ crucified and risen and the colossal implications in concrete human living, personal and domestic, local and national, political and economic, international and interracial, of that definitive revelation of the mind and love of God.

12

AFRICAN INDEPENDENCY

There is nothing new in the fact of independency. The multiplication of separate churches has been a repeated characteristic of the christian tradition, above all since the sixteenth century. It can be seen as a mark of religious vitality and its emergence in Africa during this century might be taken to show that Africa is taking christianity seriously—as seriously as did sixteenth-century Europe or seventeenth-century England. Nevertheless the scale of the movement is new. In Africa today there are not scores of separate churches, but hundreds, even thousands. Moreover it is, I think, new—at least to any very great extent—in happening within a missionary situation. This is not the breaking apart of old churches, but an almost instantaneous effect of large-scale church missionary activity.

Despite the very extensive, and rapidly growing, literature which now exists on these churches, we remain much in the dark about them. We do not even, and really cannot, know how many there are, or how many adherents they have, though the first cannot be less than several thousands and the second than six million. The most detailed general survey is that of David Barrett, who estimated 5,031 distinct bodies and 6,868,800 adherents,[1] the last figure including children. Yet what figures do exist do not relate to any one date. If it is extremely difficult to obtain at all reliable figures for the mission churches with their fairly systematic organisation, it is generally quite impossible to do so for

1 D. Barrett, *Schism and Renewal in Africa*, Oxford (OUP) 1968, 79.

these mostly far less structured bodies.[2] Moreover their rise is often better documented than their decline. Nearly one-tenth of all christians in Africa today may belong to independent churches, that is churches which came into existence without any overseas connection.[3] What is undeniable is the general size and significance of the movement. By far its greatest spread is in South Africa, where three million members and over two thousand separate bodies is certainly a minimum estimate, but it is also very strong in Rhodesia, Kenya, Nigeria and Congo-Kinshasa. It is present to some degree in almost every African country.

The diversity among these bodies is enormous: in size, from a score or two of members to tens of thousands; in origin, from a minority which made a clear break-away from a mission to the many others which represent a further split within an existing independent church or, again, a quite new body called into existence by a prophet; in stability, from a passing group of malcontents to a well organised society with a disciplined ministry and a history of several decades; in doctrine and worship, from some which have maintained a pattern of belief and practice largely inherited from western missionaries to others which are far more original and deeply African; in vitality, from some which remain a small closed-in village sect of elderly people to others which are quickly expanding, inter-tribal, even international; in education, from the majority whose leaders are

2 There are exceptions. The African Israel Church Nineveh in Western Kenya, for instance, keeps very careful records of church membership, see F. Welbourn and B. Ogot, *A Place to Feel at Home*, Oxford (OUP) 1966, 84.

3 Professor Mbiti in *African Religions and Philosophy*, 1969, 232, writes 'At least one-fifth of the christians of Africa belong to these independent churches'. This would appear to be a considerable exaggeration. David Barrett, *International Review of Mission*, January 1970, pages 41 and 47, puts it at just under 10% and seems to think this percentage will remain fairly constant. For 1970 he estimates 8·7 million independent adherents in a total sub-Saharan christian population (according to church statistics) of 90·1 million.

of very limited education to some whose leaders have a considerable western type training.

In many parts of Africa, despite obvious limitations, these churches certainly manifest an indigenisation of christianity, a locally based dynamism, and the emergence of spiritual leaders of great power, which should be the envy of the mission churches, which too often (and particularly in the case of the Catholic Church) still manifest an extremely foreign appearance and a predominant dependence upon overseas money and personnel.

The last dozen years have seen the publication of a very extensive literature on the subject, of which the most valuable pieces are monographs on particular churches or a group of churches in a given area. There have also been a number of important more general studies, in particular those of Sundkler, Barrett and Oosthuizen.[4] To produce any sort of general assessment at this stage is not easy and I feel that both Oosthuizen and Barrett have given way to the danger of allowing their closer knowledge of a very particular area or church (in one case the Zulu Nazarite church of Isaiah Shembe, in the other the Luo churches in Kenya) to dominate their general interpretation of a continent-wide phenomenon. All three more general books are of real value, but one must insist that there is no reason to believe that there is one over-riding cause behind, or a single pattern in, these many movements. The fundamental reasons for separation from a mission church or the emergence of a new group in some other way can in one case be social or political, in another express a theological vision, in a third relate to what are regarded as unsatisfactory structures in a mission church, or again concern chiefly the character of a particular individual.

The present study is no more than a tentative attempt to

4 B. Sundkler, *Bantu Prophets in South Africa*, 2nd edition, Oxford 1961. Barrett, op. cit.; G. C. Oosthuizen, *Post-Christianity in Africa*, London (C. Hurst) 1968.

describe and evaluate the movement as a whole in the light of recent literature.

A first question that inevitably presents itself is a typology of these groups. Following Sundkler, as modified in the second edition of *Bantu Prophets*,[5] and H. W. Turner,[6] we may say that they can, very roughly, be divided according to three chief types: Firstly, groups which have retained the main characteristics of the mission churches in doctrine, liturgy and organisation (at times, indeed with a severe conservatism) but have divided on personal or racial grounds (often as a reaction to some form of missionary paternalism). In South Africa these have come to be known as 'Ethiopian',[7] in Nigeria as 'African'[8] churches. Equally, from a general western (more Protestant) viewpoint they could be termed substantially 'orthodox'.

Secondly, there are those groups whose independence goes with deeply different forms of worship, organisation and belief. They have generally been founded by a 'prophet' with greater or less charismatic power and they seldom represent the breaking away of a group as such from a mission church; they concentrate largely upon the cure of the sick through prayer. Historically, they are as a movement rather more recent in origin than the first group. In South Africa American Zionism had an influence upon the beginnings of this movement and the whole movement has there come to be known as 'Zionist'. In Nigeria they are known as 'Aladura' (praying) churches, and in West Africa generally as 'spiritual' churches.[9] Much more evidently and profoundly Africanised than the first group, they still retain

5 pp. 5, 53–59, 323–337.

6 *African Independent Church*, Oxford 1967, II, xiii–xviii.

7 For the various uses of this name see G. Shepperson, *Ethiopianism: Past and Present*, in C. G. Baeta, ed. *Christianity in Tropical Africa*, Oxford 1968, 249–264.

8 For a study of these see J. B. Webster's *The African Churches among the Yoruba 1888–1922*, Oxford 1964.

9 For Aladura see H. W. Turner, op. cit., and J. Peel, *Aladura*, Oxford (OUP) 1968.

the central christian beliefs. Some could be classified (and classify themselves[10]) as Pentecostal. While the first group represent in large measure a direct reaction to a certain racialism in mission policy, this group—while its direct connections with mission churches are smaller—may represent a criticism of the growing secularism in the work of the mission churches after the 1920s. This can be particularly true in West Africa. While the missions have concentrated upon schools and their priests have come to be known as 'managers', the Aladura churches have concentrated upon prayer.

It may be noted here that many Zionist and Ethiopian churches fully admit polygamy, at least for the laity; however it is equally true that there are others which are quite strongly anti-polygamous. Some, while allowing polygamy to the laity, insist upon monogamy for the clergy on account of the clear ruling in 1 Tim 3:2 and 12.

Thirdly, there is the syncretistic and messianic group (called by some 'nativistic'). It is only recently that it has been realised that this is truly a different category from the second, even though many of their lesser though often striking characteristics—for instance the establishment of a central sacred village where the founder may be buried—are often the same. But a messiah-type of founder is theologically quite different from a prophet-type. One substantially replaces Christ, the other does not. In these bodies there is also a very substantial mixing of christian (or, to a large extent, Old Testament) motifs with traditional African ones. The christian character of the whole is no longer clear. This group appears to be much smaller than the others. One of its best known examples is the ama-Nazaretha, the Nazarite Church founded in Natal by Isaiah Shembe in 1911.[11] Another is the Zambian Lumpa Church of Alice Lenshina.

[10] For instance the Christ Apostolic Church in Nigeria, Peel, op. cit., p. 148.
[11] Much information on this church is to be found in Sundkler,

None of these movements, as regards their general classification, is really unique to Africa, and they certainly need to be understood within the wider vistas of church history. If the rapidity of their growth seems fairly unique, it must again be seen within the rapidity of growth of the mission churches themselves in Africa in this century. If there has never been a comparably rapid movement of multiple independency, there has also never been a comparably rapid movement of multiple church growth of an extensionist missionary kind.

Movements of this sort and the fascination they exercise on their adherents are sometimes misunderstood because their specifically religious content, their spiritual and theological stresses are not given adequate weight. Four particular types of religious pressure and motivation may be instanced here. None is specifically African, but that they are strongly present in many of these movements cannot be doubted. The first is the call of perfectionism: the elitist group with its own stringent rules of behaviour, morals or ritual behaviour, very probably with the sense of being at odds with the rest of the world. This is the real sense of sect. Such a church insists on a very exact conformity, but acceptance of it means an unquestioned sharing with the saints and deliverance from the world. Persecution can be a need for this type of group.

The second is the strongly Old Testament orientated church. The bible is unequivocally the word of God right through. The Old Testament is put on a par with the New, and it is found to be condemnable that christians habitually ignore so many of its precepts. Sabbatarianism is one instance of this. There is a constant christian tendency, noticeable particularly in circles coming under Calvinist influence, to hark back to a rather literal application of

op. cit. G. C. Oosthuizen has devoted a monograph to the thought of its founder: *The Theology of a South African Messiah*, E. J. Brill, Leiden, 1967; there is also much on the topic in his wider work *Post-Christianity in Africa*.

Old Testament commands and attitudes. This is the more attractive when many of them seem rather close to traditional African practice.

The third is the Pentecostal approach: the call to partake in a manifest revival of the Spirit gifts of the early church. In age after age this appears as a theme of christian renewal. Prophecy, the gift of tongues, shaking and quaking, are characteristics of modern African churches just as they were of many English seventeenth century ones.

The fourth is some form of millennialism, the expectation of a rapidly coming apocalyptic end to normal society and its replacement by a new order in which the group of believers will alone participate or at least enjoy a highly privileged position. Imminent eschatological expectations inevitably affect one's general behaviour and order of priorities. This point of view is central for the Jehovah's Witnesses (strong in Zambia and Malawi) who have many of the characteristics of independency, and for some of the messianic groups. Parts of the New Testament eschatology suggest such immediacy as to make this type of approach very understandable for those who take the scriptures seriously, but it is also true that many of the millennialists are not basically christian.

It is chiefly the millennialist groups which tend to come into conflict with government, and especially with young nationalist governments which have their own implicit secular millennialism; but the vast majority of African independent movements are not millennialist and have few immediate political implications.[12]

These four attitudes can, of course, greatly overlap; when christian, they all share in a common fundamentalism, to which indeed the only alternative is in the end a full acceptance of integral development in christian life and

12 For millennialism see S. L. Thrupp (ed.) *Millennial Dreams in Action*, the Hague 1962, and Bryan Wilson, *Millennialism in Comparative Perspective*, Comparative Studies in Society and History, October 1963, 93-114.

thought. But an ecclesiology with a built-in theory of development is a much more subtle thing to justify scripturally than an ecclesiology which is stridently fundamentalist. The trouble with the latter, of course, is that the more fundamentalist one is, the more partial one must also be, effectively appealing to only certain chosen sections of the bible. Certainly the vernacular bible and a rather fundamentalist way of interpreting it—and christians after all vary only in the degree of their fundamentalism—present the springboard for independency, both African and otherwise.

But in Africa more than elsewhere christianity has come into very close contact on a large scale with non-christian religions. The very rapidity of church expansion has meant the massive absorption into the christian community of people still largely influenced by other religious viewpoints. These other religious forces are often much deeper in the person than the christian tenets he has recently learnt and they may even control the way in which the latter are interpreted. They are, after all, connatural with his language, which christianity, at least in the first generation, is not.

This inevitably produces a personal syncretism in many members of mission controlled churches and an institutionalised syncretism in independent churches. This is particularly easy as so many members of the latter—probably the great majority—were never full members of a mission church but, if anything, peripheral members, many unbaptised. It is particularly (though far from only) to those people who have in some way identified themselves with a mission church and would call themselves christian, but have failed to complete a period of catechumenate, that the independent movements appeal. It is further true that some separatist churches have a powerful missionary sense and in some areas have converted very many people direct from paganism. As the ministerial training in most such churches is still practically nil, the possibilities for extensive instruction of neophytes are also highly limited. Again, this can result in a high degree of 'passing across' of pagan attitudes into a christian body.

In some ways the Old Testament is a bridge between paganism and christianity. Africans find prescriptions in the Old Testament, for instance with regard to food and dress, similar to customs they have formerly practised; again, the Old Testament offers good precedents for polygamy. It is sometimes not clear as a consequence whether in its ways of believing and practice an independent church should be classified as 'nativistic' or as 'Old Testament inclined'. Very many attach an exceptional importance to Moses, just as John the Baptist often tends to be the New Testament figure to whom most attention is paid, while Paul is ignored or even criticised.

All this being said, it remains true that the more African independency is studied, the more the truly syncretic forms appear of rather marginal importance. The great majority of churches in South, West and East can without much doubt be fairly classified as christian. Sundkler detected evidence some years ago of a tendency of breakaway churches to become more syncretistic as the years passed, and to return from schism to paganism[13]; but there is also increasing evidence of an opposite trend of the larger churches at least to grow purer as the years go by, steadily weeding out the elements in their practice which appear to be less compatible with traditional christianity.[14]

It is impossible to evaluate properly the religious and theological factors behind African independency without consideration of the difference in impact of Protestant and Catholic missionaries. Protestant missionary work was far

[13] Sundkler, op. cit., p. 297.

[14] Turner, op. cit. One senses that in 'the Church of the Lord' which he describes Emmanuel Adejobi, its second primate, has a markedly clearer doctrinal sense than Josiah Oshitele, the founder; cf also the study on Kimbanguism of M. L. Martin, *Prophetic Christianity in the Congo*, pp. 10, 16, 38.

more developed and effective in Africa in the nineteenth century particularly in those parts where such work was able to begin really early—South Africa and parts of the west coast. The whole subsequent process of church growth and the tensions which this can produce between missionaries and local people were as a result experienced by Protestants well in advance of Catholics. But the contrast between the two was not merely one of timing. Evidently there have been very big differences of aim and practice between different Protestant missionary bodies, but in general their teaching inevitably implied far more than the Catholic the right of the local church to direct itself in freedom; further, in most places Protestant bodies developed a local ordained ministry—with a rather limited education—far more energetically than did Catholics; thirdly, they did far more in the line of bible translation. These three points all have significance in the development of independency. With such ecclesiology as they had Protestants were far less able than Catholics to justify a semi-permanent retention of church control in the hands of foreign missionaries, and yet in practice until very far into the twentieth century they hung on to control just as much. Their more rapid ordination of local men was bound to produce leaders who would chafe bitterly at this retention; finally, the translation of the bible placed in African hands criteria for judging the whole concrete way of christian living they had been brought. Why prefer the practice of the missionaries to the word of God? The tension could be particularly acute where there were several Protestant denominations working in a single area. Their disagreement upon relatively minor points and consequent division went far to justify local christians too in establishing yet more communions.[15]

15 So R. L. Wishlade remarks: 'The fact that in the single administrative District of Mlanje no fewer than eleven White missions are operating provides ample precedents for further African secessions', *Sectarianism in Southern Nyasaland*, Oxford 1965, p. 143.

It is not too difficult then to understand why the vast majority of schisms in Africa have come from Protestant churches—particularly Methodists, Baptists and Low Church Anglicans.[16] It is perfectly true that of recent years there have also been a number of break-aways from Catholicism, of which the biggest has been the 'Maria Legio' in Kenya.[17] There has also been the 'Bana ba mutima' or Sacred Heart Church[18] in Zambia and several in the Congo. It is true also that many Catholics afterwards join an established independent church—doubtless many of them peripheral Catholics. Movements like the Bamalaki in Uganda fifty years ago and the Lumpa Church in Northern Rhodesia ten years ago carried away (largely temporarily) thousands of Catholic catechumens and many also of the baptised. Yet there can be no doubt of the very wide difference between Catholic and Protestant missions in this regard, a difference which is enormous indeed when one considers how many times larger the Catholic community is than any one other communion. One may even point out that when a major schism such as that of the Legio has come from Roman Catholicism, it has come in a tribe where independency from Protestant sources has already become commonplace and so somehow prepared the ground.

Basic to this difference appears to me to be the inherent ecclesiology of Protestant bodies which cannot but go a long way to justifying further secessions on serious grounds. If African christians are willing to protest and to secede, Protestant missionaries might reasonably congratulate themselves on having put across an intrinsic element of their own tradition: an ability and a confidence to judge of their own church in freedom.

---

16 It is interesting to note that while the Anglican CMS (Evangelical) has provided the material for a particularly large number of schisms, the UMCA (Anglo-Catholic) has, I believe, produced none at all.

17 For the Maria Legio see P. J. Dirven, MHM, *A Protest and a Challenge*, AFER 1970, pp. 127–136.

18 This appears now to be nearly defunct.

Secondly, the worshipping needs of African people seem often very inadequately satisfied by austere Protestant services. Dr Sundkler has remarked that 'Protestant Missions brought the Zulus into contact with a form of Christianity which was centred round a Book. The independent church changed the stress and evolved a form of religion centred round a set of rites.'[19] The same tendency has manifested itself in every side of the continent: seceders from Presbyterianism. Congregationalism, Low Church Anglicanism frequently (though certainly not always) adopt liturgical practices of a Catholic character and make of ritual rather than reading the heart of their religious practice. Certainly this should help to explain why there have been fewer schisms from Catholicism; in the latter Africans have often encountered something of that sense of the sacred, of mystery, of a rich not too well understood liturgy which they thirsted for in vain in Protestant churches. This does not, of course, mean that traditional Catholic ritual was fully satisfactory for African worshipping needs. That is far from the case, and the independent churches have often developed a very different kind of ritual of their own, in the lines of communal praying, singing and dancing, and especially in extensive blessings for the sick. Nevertheless the difference in the use of ritually expressed symbols between traditional Catholic and traditional Protestant worship, as introduced by missionaries, has been a significant one.

This goes, I think, with a widespread sense that the Catholic Church is somehow particularly authentic in the line of church. In this connection a remark of the founder of the Ruponeso Church in Rhodesia is worth quoting. He himself was formerly a member of the Dutch Reformed Church and he was justifying the adoption of Catholic ritual practices in his own body: 'The Catholic Church is the father and mother of all churches. You are our big

19 *Bantu Prophets in South Africa*, p. 181.

king, and this is why we imitate you.'[20] Such an attitude
makes schism from the Catholic Church less likely.

Thirdly, the influence of the bible goes far to explain
why the atmosphere in Protestant churches can be more
favourable to schism. It is to be particularly connected with
the translation of the Old Testament. African Protestants
have often been offered the bible without any adequate
balancing ecclesiology. Few African Catholics, on the other
hand, have until these last years come into much close contact with the Old Testament. Their knowledge of it has
been carefully mediated via the clergy. What they have had
of scripture they have had flanked by a strong doctrine of
the church. They have never possessed the bible as an
ostensibly independent source of authority, something
whereby they could easily judge missionaries. This is
undoubtedly important, and yet I do not believe that the
fact and extent of scripture translation can possibly be regarded alone as a near adequate explanation for the
growth of schism. In important countries, such as Tanzania
and Uganda, where the bible has long been translated into
many languages, independency has been a consistent failure.[21] What one can say is that where there are other strong
factors making for schism, the presence of the bible in the
vernacular has been important in providing a rationale
within a Protestant context for the action of breaking
apart.

Fourthly, the whole Catholic attitude to ministerial training has, I think, helped to discourage fission. In the words
of a writer speaking of southern Malawi,

A person cannot appoint himself a Catholic priest, but
he can appoint himself a Protestant minister without
running counter to the main doctrinal tenets held by the

[20] M. Aquina OP, 'Christianity in a Rhodesian Tribal Trust Land'
in *African Social Research* (University of Zambia), June 1966, 33.
[21] For Uganda see F. B. Welbourn *East African Rebels*, SCM 1961;
for Tanzania T. Ranger *The African Churches of Tanzania*, East
African Publishing House 1969.

Protestant missions operating in Mlanje. In the Protestant churches and sects, unlike the Catholic Church,
no elaborate ritual surrounds the appointment of its
officials and they are not regarded as part of an unbroken
chain of authority. There are already many similar Protestant hierarchies and a person seceeding from one of
them can attempt to create a structural replica of the
parent body from which he has seceded; this he cannot
do in the Catholic Church.[22]

The theology learnt, the way of life practised, the status inherent in the Catholic priesthood, all militate against
secession.

These are religious and ecclesiastical factors making for
and against schism. African independency as a whole cannot, however, be explained purely or even pre-eminently
in theological terms. The stark fact is that well over half
of both the separated bodies and their adherents lie in two
countries: South Africa and Rhodesia. It is almost impossible not to connect this very closely with the socio-political
situation in these settler lands with their racialist policies.
It has been the colour-bar practised both in society as
a whole and even within the life of the church that has
acted as an enormous stimulus to the formation of christian
churches in which there will be no white top dog. Nevertheless one must be careful here: apartheid is not the only
special characteristic of South African society. Another is
the extent of urbanisation of uneducated people. The old
society is broken up, tens of thousands of people are flung
into a new type of society without any extensive new kind
of education, and in the great social and psychological insecurity in which they find themselves they turn to a
religious group which is somehow new, a part of this new
world, yet to which they feel that they can fully belong,
something their own. In the long run independency seems
to flourish more in the town than in the country, though

22 Wishlade, op. cit, p. 99.

it appeals rather little to people with secondary education and in the higher income groups, who prefer one of the historic churches. In shanty towns and many other better constructed high density residential areas, both in South Africa and in countries to the north, the mission churches are often most inadequately represented, if at all. Traditional religion does not, of course, necessarily die out by any means. On the contrary there may be more call on the diviner's art in the town than in the country. Yet the milieu is so different and so many of the pressures new that they promote the seeking of new religious allegiances.

The South African social situation also encourages religious independency by its relative lack of openings for leadership in other directions. The outlawing of effective political and trade union activity is a strong stimulus to religious activity. The independent churches may indeed be seen by the government as a safety valve for letting off leadership steam in a rather innocuous way. Only in rather few cases, of which that of John Chilembwe of Nyasaland was the most striking, did ecclesiastical independency appear to have political implications in a colonial situation; and where there was some connection the link has weakened since the coming of political independence.[23] Furthermore, there has, I think, been a definite decline in independent religious activity in the years following political independence. Kenya seems to offer an exception to this, but even that could be partly explained by the fact that the tribes chiefly concerned, notably the Luo, may feel that they have had less than their fair share of the fruits of political independence; while for the Kikuyu in the post-independence period the mission-connected churches have shown a new attractiveness. In general it must be remem-

[23] For the relation between independent churches and politics reference should be made to the very balanced study of H. W. Turner, 'The Place of the Religious Movements in the Modernization of Africa', *Journal of Religion in Africa* (Brill, Leiden), vol. II, fasc. 1 (1969), 43–63.

bered that religious independency, in appealing particularly to the lower educated groups, has its constituency among people who have anyway little hope of obtaining the loaves and fishes even in an independent country. Today as much as ever there are two Nairobis.

It is clear that the social factors behind independency are much more complex than a simple equation with the presence of a colour-bar and white settlement. There has been far too much independency in West Africa, particularly in Nigeria and Ghana, for that to hold water as anything like a complete explanation.[24] Nevertheless even in West Africa there was in fact a practical colour-bar within the mission churches from the point of view of leadership positions in the half century following 1890. This is a point of the greatest importance. A situation in which a mission church has already made considerable progress and a lower locally recruited ministerial hierarchy has been established but in which the door seems closed to native promotion at higher levels is an ideal one for stimulating schism, and such was the position of most Protestant churches in, for instance, western Nigeria about 1900.[25] Of course, once one or two separatist churches have been established in an area or a tribe, and seem to be a success, the idea naturally takes on and spreads. Catholic missions did not for many years reach a point in which this sort of frustration was widely felt, though it was certainly growing strong in a number of countries in the years 1935–55.

It is to be noted that the social factors behind independency are not all related to the phenomenon of colonialism: the traditional structures of a particular tribe are also important. Thus the whole authority pattern of the Baganda made for the acceptance of the christian church in Anglican or Catholic form with a pronounced stress upon hierarchy.

[24] For Nigeria see the works of Turner, Webster and Peel already cited; for Ghana, C. G. Baeta *Prophetism in Ghana*, London (SCM Press) 1962.
[25] See Webster, op. cit., throughout.

On the other hand, the absence of similar political structures among the Luo, their tendency to organise in small
independent groups politically and commercially, their
openness to charismatic leadership, all help to explain the
Luo proneness to independent churchmanship. Again there
are serious social and psychological problems with which,
from an African viewpoint, the mission churches fail to
cope adequately. One is certainly the failure to offer any
treatment for sickness which does not include payment for
medicines and travelling, possibly, miles to a hospital or
dispensary. Another is the problem of witchcraft, sorcery,
the interference of evil spirits. Most missionaries are themselves not sufficiently preoccupied with such things to be of
real help to people who are deadly sure they suffer from
them. Many independent churches help people in these circumstances just because they take them seriously.

To conclude this general discussion on the factors making
for independency in Africa during the last eighty years, I
would list ten chief ones. First of all, a missionary outlook
and theology which somehow provided justification for
secession.[26] Secondly, the multiplication of Protestant missions within a single area. This is very obvious for much of
South Africa, Malawi, western Nigeria and western Kenya.
Equally, the absence of much overlapping of Protestant
missions is striking for Uganda, Tanzania, Rwanda and
Burundi, where independency is also largely lacking.
Thirdly, lack of scope in the life of some mission churches
for ritual and a concretisation of the sacral. Fourthly, the
need for small worshipping neighbourhood groups to give
a sense of security, togetherness and shared communal
prayer which mission churches, with their large buildings
and rather small number of ordained ministers, lack.[27]

[26] Joseph Booth, responsible in one way or another for so many of
the independent churches of southern Malawi, is a particularly good
example of this, see G. Shepperson and T. Price *Independent African*,
Edinburgh University Press, 1958.

[27] See an article in *Herder Correspondence*, November 1968.

Fifthly, a pattern of tribal life encouraging decentralisation and fission. Sixthly, areas of felt need for which the mission churches make little provision. Seventhly, a bar to the senior promotion of native ministers within a white dominated church. Eighthly, a wider colour bar in society operating also to a greater or lesser extent within the general life of the established churches. Ninthly, the disorientation that goes with rapid social change and gives a particular insecurity to the less educated within an urban situation. Tenthly, lack of scope for African leadership and initiative within the political, civic and industrial fields.

These factors must be taken as operating in a cumulative way. Every one of them has been present in South Africa; a lesser but still considerable number in Kenya or Zambia; almost none in Tanzania or Rwanda. Some can fade away with a change of government and a change also in missionary policy, as has happened strikingly in many places in the last decade. Such changes may produce—and indeed in some places appear to be already producing—a relative diminution in the dynamism of independency. But the range of reasons does show what a very complicated phenomenon this is.

In both south and West Africa the independent movement began with the establishment of 'Ethiopian' or 'African' churches, while later on interest moved to the founding of 'Zionist' or 'Aladura' churches. The others, of course, continued to grow, but in West Africa new ones were seldom formed. Thus in Nigeria the period for the establishment of 'African churches' was between 1885 and 1925, while that in which the spiritual churches were mostly inaugurated was 1910 to 1950. So Webster writes,

Since the majority of the non-Yoruba areas of Nigeria unfortunately missed the stimulus of nineteenth-century mission policies, so also they have missed the African Church Movement, which was a product of the thought of that age. It is noteworthy that the African church has flourished best in those areas where evangelisation was well under way in the nineteenth century, Calabar, the Niger Delta, and Yorubaland. Elsewhere the African churches have branches, but they cannot be said to profoundly influence the Christian situation.[28]

Turner remarks on the subject of the rise of new spiritual churches, 'one wonders if the day for the development of new aladura churches on this scale has now passed'.[29] Particular forms of independency result from a particular historical situation which only lasts for a certain length of time. The opportune time for the initiation of such movements both began later and is probably ending later in eastern Africa than in West Africa, but in the east too it may well be almost over now. In South Africa, where the social and political situation is utterly different and the number of individuals involved is also far greater, new churches of all types continue to be founded.

We have frequently to remind ourselves that the great majority of African christians have been, and remain, finally content to belong to a mission-connected church. Only in South Africa is it distinctly possible that this may not continue to be the case in the forseeable future. Those who have broken away (at least in the case of 'Ethiopian' or 'African' churches) have done so in positive or negative protest at the way mission churches were run by foreigners or—occasionally—by too foreign-minded Africans. The more the mission churches are completely taken over as regards their leadership positions by Africans and the more they are willing to adapt themselves in other ways to African culture, the less likely is it that further separatist movements on a large scale will take place.

Relative to the total size of the christian body, the independent churches may be decreasing today in a number of

[28] Webster, op. cit., p. 197.

[29] H. W. Turner, op. cit., I, p. 101. Existing aladura churches are, however, continuing to grow extremely fast, see Peel *Aladura*, pp. 218–229.

African countries. However, in other countries and for those bodies which are already well established the case is very different. What is happening here is in part a process of becoming more respectable and of assimilation to the mission-connected churches. When the latter too are in some way Africanised differences naturally decrease, particularly with those independent churches which always cherished the general doctrinal and worshipping pattern of their parent body. In many parts of the continent today independent churches are applying for membership of local christian councils, they are endeavouring to raise the standards of their ministerial training and even sending ministers for instruction in theological colleges directed by mission churches; they are again attempting to build up overseas contacts which can provide a sense of wider communion and provide financial assistance. In South Africa 261 churches now belong to AICA (the African Independent Churches' Association) and the Christian Institute is assisting them in organising both long and short courses of ministerial training. In this process there tends too to be a certain ironing out of differences between the Ethiopian and Zionist groups, the doctrinal position of the latter being often extremely flexible. At the same time, as the young church is more widely recognised in ecclesiastical circles and its ministers receive more training, its acceptability to the educated laity increases. The children of Zionists going to secondary school have a greater probability of remaining Zionists. The Christ Apostolic Church in Nigeria even maintains an impressive number of schools of its own. So the present time appears to be no longer so much a period of creative new beginnings as of consolidation. Doubtless many small churches are not capable of this; some simply melt away as their average age advances, others are continually weakened by leadership conflicts and internal schisms.

From one point of view their challenge to the mission-connected churches outside South Africa may seem to be less today than it was a few years ago. As already remarked, in all other countries the majority of christians clearly prefer to remain in a church with overseas connections and, perhaps, the respectability that comes from operating major institutions. In comparison, most independent churches offer an experience which, if intimate, is also narrow, frequently tribalistic and rather non-intellectual. Many independent churches in a post-colonial Africa suffer from lack of adequate organisation to maintain earlier advances, lack of an even remotely educated leadership, lack maybe of any clear raison d'être. They remain a refuge for the elderly and the uneducated and tend to be broken up by frequent further divisions. The educated man brought up in a Catholic or an Anglican school and seeing today an African archbishop at the head of the church in his country is quite unlikely to be drawn towards independency.

From other points of view one may judge somewhat differently. For one thing, the independent churches are for the most part 'africanised' in a far deeper and more convincing way than is normal with the mission churches, and they seem to be exerting their appeal particularly in parts of the continent which are today also in other fields culturally dynamic. For another, this appeal remains particularly attractive to the poorer classes in the new urban and peri-urban areas. These are people whom the mission churches are largely failing to reach, and the very inadequate numbers of their ordained ministers and rather rigid church structures do not help them here. This is particularly true of the Catholic Church and of parts like Kenya and western Nigeria where independency is rife and there are singularly few African Catholic priests.[30] In most parts of Africa it is still true that the Catholic Church in particular is deaf to the call of the big towns. The independent churches have a flexibility which enables them to make much progress among the new urban proletariat with

[30] For independency in Kenya see Welbourn and Ogot, *A Place to feel at home*, Oxford 1966; part III of Welbourn *East African Rebels*, London (scm Press) 1961; also the article of Dirven already cited.

whom their ministers share an economic level. At the same time the consolidating process already spoken of makes it likely that as the education of the people rises, so will the status and pastoral resources of independency. Certainly in Kenya and Yorubaland the future dominant pattern of church adherence is as yet anything but clear.

The intrinsic value in many of these movements should be evident. They are sincerely religious and christian, even though there are things in their practices and belief that one may regret. Where both independent and mission churches are present the former, at least at times, may realise a deeper and more genuine life of prayer and spiritual community than the latter. Moreover, in many places they offer today a possibility of christian living to many people the mission churches could not reach at all. They have built up little christian communities in township areas of Moslem West Africa where the missions have never established themselves at all. Moreover the intellectualism, ecclesiastical rigidity, personal authoritarianism and sheer foreignness of much western missionary work simply forced an explosion of this kind, greatly assisted by the social and political situation in countries like South Africa, Rhodesia and Kenya. In many cases they offer a genuine indictment of major aspects of missionary activity, but in many others they simply show that evangelism and church planting are very much more complex processes than the honest but simple missionary (or even missionary theorist) imagined. The consequences of cultural contact and religious conversion can be many and some of them seemingly very queer. Certainly in general missionaries tended to impose too much and allow too small a sphere of freedom; they seldom anticipated that the Spirit might speak directly to their converts, that their converts might even see things—christian things—to which they themselves had been blind. There was small room in their well ordered compounds for men with the charismatic gifts of a William Harris, a Josiah Oshitele, a Simon Kimbangu.

For those within the Catholic Church the challenges all

this appears to offer are: first, how to reconcile unity with diversity: that is to say, how within the context of Catholic communion to liberate the forces that can bring about a genuine africanisation and localisation of the church's message, pattern of life, ministry and worship in ways more radical than most of us have dared to attempt or indeed most seminary-trained priests, African or otherwise, are willing to envisage for an instant; secondly, how to stimulate christian community within the less affluent urban context; thirdly, how in South Africa to rid the Catholic Church of the image of white domination it at present possesses.

The Roman Catholic Church in Africa is today a dinosaur kept on its legs with annual blood transfusions of men and money from Europe and North America. In the coming years, as those blood transfusions steadily diminish, how will that dinosaur compete with this multitude of little home-grown churches? The answer to that will, I believe, depend very greatly on the extent to which in each country Catholics take these warnings sincerely to heart and to the undoubted appeal of a universal communion, an intellectual gospel and a rich liturgy add a new indigeneity of expression, personnel and support, a far greater awareness of the spiritual, social and psychological needs of urban man, and a pattern of ministry adapted both to the countryside and to the town which will make of the small worshipping and serving community not only an independent but also a Catholic reality.